"*Healing Wounded Emotions* distills 20 years of experience in counseling into practical help."

Publisher's Weekly

"...a remarkably helpful and thoughtful book."

Thomas More Book Club

"Padovani's aim is to foster a better understanding between the human and spiritual dynamics, for in that lies a wealth of human potential."

Catholic Twin Circle

"Everyone has problems! How we deal with them—coping or being overcome—is an indication of our strength and faith. An aim of *Healing Wounded Emotions* is to dispel the erroneous notions concerning fundamental aspects of the human person. Christianity and psychology meet in the person, not to dichotomize, but to enrich. From this basis, Padovani puts forth his two-fold premise—a sense of personal worth and responsibility....Persons burdened by difficulties in life can achieve new freedom by ascribing to the author's message....Without question, *Healing Wounded Emotions* is recommended."

Rev. Jay C. Haskin
The Vermont Catholic Tribune

"The material in this book is sound clinically and theologically, its advice filled with wisdom and sensitivity, its composition compelling and poetic."

James Reed
Toronto School of Theology

"Let this book by priest-counselor Martin Padovani show you how to put conflicting emotions to rest, so you can overcome life's hurts and live more freely, more fully."

Praying

"Father Padovani...structures his book around two main themes: the need for people to develop a sense of personal worth and their need to be willing to accept personal responsibility for their actions and lives....he discusses such emotions as anger, guilt, depression, self-criticism, and self-love, and how they affect people's lives as Christians."

Faith Today
NC News Service

"A resource for human growth that will be of special value in helping people better understand their emotional and spiritual dimensions. Persons with psychological and religious conflicts will find guidance and clarification to remove unnecessary guilt and foster peace. Anyone involved in counseling others will find this book a valuable handbook."

Alive & Well & Living in New York City

"Fr. Padovani has written a superb book, which is a welcome addition to many recent works attempting to integrate psychological theory with Christian values and theology. The information is clinically helpful and psychologically sound. It cuts across the major issues pastoral counselors and pastoral care professionals are likely to encounter."

Richard Glenn
Health Progress

HEALING Wounded EMOTIONS

OVERCOMING LIFE'S HURTS

MARTIN H. PADOVANI

Foreword by John Powell, sj

TWENTY-THIRD PUBLICATIONS
Mystic, Connecticut

Twelfth printing 1995

Twenty-Third Publications
185 Willow Street
P.O. Box 180
Mystic, CT 06355
(203) 536-2611
800-321-0411

ISBN 0-89622-333-7
Library of Congress Catalog Number 86-51614
Printed in the U.S.A.

Foreword

Viktor Frankl once observed that psychology has spent the last fifty years in an excessively narrow preoccupation. It has focused its attention almost exclusively on the human mind and body. He expressed the hope that the next fifty years would include equal time for the neglected human spirit. We know what happens when the mind or body is deprived of needed nourishment. Almost strangely, however, we have ignored the hungry human spirit. We have been selectively silent about the persistent questions of the human spirit: questions about where we have come from, what are we doing, and where we are going. Body and mind certainly, but also the spirit, are all essential, interrelated and interacting parts of our human nature.

We as humans are not simply disengaged spirits, souls in need of saving. We are also mind and body, and we are going to have a bumpy ride through life if we try to be spiritual without also trying to be human. Theology must somehow include a consideration of the human just as a true psychology must also attend to the spiritual part of the human composite.

So it is very refreshing to come upon a book like the one in your hands. In these essays, Martin Padovani helps us see ourselves in all three dimensions: body, mind, and spirit. He helps us understand the necessary compatibility between psychology and faith. He speaks of a religious faith that is helpful, one that integrates feelings and faith into a total human harmony. He warns us against a religious faith that can be harmful.

There is much food for thought here. It is a book that should be processed, discussed in a group, or used as a basis for a personal journal. Like the author, I too see much human suffering as "needless." I see a backlog of unexpressed feelings imprisoning tortured human beings. I see people trying to be religious without an equal effort to be human. And, of course, I see people trying to be human as though psychology alone were a sufficient savior. Both delusions can result only in sadness and disappointment.

Two of Martin Padovani's themes, brilliantly described in these pages, are like the two legs on which we humans walk across the face of this earth on our life-journey to God's house. The first is *a sense of personal worth,* which is the backbone of human identity and the essential foundation of human happiness. The second is a *a sense of personal responsibility.* In this context I have often thought of us humans as either "owners" or "blamers." We either accept a personal responsibility for our lives, by owning our actions and reactions, or we blame them on others.

Owners get in touch with their own inner spaces. Blamers go through life setting up and knocking down "straw men." Blamers suffer a kind of human exhaustion in their persistent avoidance of responsibility. They seriously limit their potential self-knowledge: they never get to know themselves.

Don't let the riches of these pages be lost. Process them in some way. The years invested by the author in counseling us troubled human beings have been for him the laboratory of life. His valuable conclusions will be helpful to us only to the extent that we digest them, that we make them our own and integrate them into our lives. I appreciate the wisdom of this book.

John Powell, S.J.
Loyola University
Chicago, Illinois

Acknowledgments

This book became possible because of the support of many people. My appreciation and gratitude go to all of them. Special thanks to Rosemary, my dedicated associate for over 20 years, for her inspiration, encouragement, and wisdom. To Fr. Patrick Connor, S.V.D., who insisted for many years that I write. When I did, he graciously accepted the laborious task of editing the manuscript with literary expertise and insightful advice. To my father, of happy memory, my mother, family, and close friends who believed in me. To all those wonderful people at Twenty-Third Publications who showed interest, enthusiasm, and the courage to publish. Finally, to the countless people who have entrusted their lives to me, and shared their sufferings in the hope of finding healing. Because of them the insights in these pages are accessible to others who also seek healing.

Contents

He has sent me to bring the good
news to those in need, and to heal
hearts that are broken.

Isaiah 61:1

AN INTERVIEW WITH THE AUTHOR

Q: What led you to write HEALING WOUNDED EMOTIONS?

Padovani: This book is partially a result of 27 years of ministering as a priest. But even more, it grows from my 19 years of counseling ministry.

Q: Has this "dual-ministry" helped you in any unique ways?

Padovani: Yes. My dual role as priest and therapist has allowed me the experience of relating to the emotional as well as the spiritual dimensions of the persons who sought counseling. Being able to deal with people in these two areas provided me with the opportunities to integrate, resolve, and coordinate these dimensions into myself, my preaching, and above all in my clients.

Q: Did people seek counseling for both kinds of problems?

Padovani: People would feel free to avail themselves of both aspects of their lives. Jung stated that under every psychological problem is a religious problem. From my ministry, I truly believe this. The nemesis with much general clinical counseling is the failure to treat the religious problems. It is equally important to ferret out the psychological problem that is often buried in every religious problem.

Q: How does this impact your more "priestly" ministry?

Padovani: I also consider the Sunday Homily as an excellent opportunity for group counseling by integrating the psychological and spiritual dimensions of the gospel message. People need to have a relevant integration of the gospel message in their human world. It also occured to me that a book of such a nature would also be a valuable source for any Christian person, especially one who is in counseling with a counselor not providing such religious information.

Q: And the book also combines these dimensions?

Padovani: Yes. It is becoming more evident to me in the face of all the tremendous and horrendous problems people are experiencing in contemporary society that people need a spiritual dimension in order to deal with them. All problems require a spiritual dimension if people are to be fully healed. My holistic approach to people, especially in counseling, has provided me with the insights that I share in this book.

Introduction

In recent years there has been an increase of writing that attempts to show the complementary and interdependent nature of the psychological and spiritual dimensions of the human person. These dimensions are not two separable aspects, but are interwoven within the human person. Each person is a psychological and spiritual being, even though the spiritual is frequently not recognized—or developed. To stress one dimension and disregard the other is to limit the understanding of both. The search for meaning and healing in our lives, indeed our ability to function in a fully human way, occurs in both parts as one influences the other. In the climate of moral confusion today, many human problems have a deep spiritual dimension, and many psychological disorders will find genuine healing only within the context of the spiritual.

For example, whatever form addictions take, they can ultimately be controlled only by a spiritual approach. Whether that spirituality involves recourse to a "higher power" or to a more defined personal God, recovering addicts attest to "the spiritual" as their only hope of survival. That is why the spiritual program of the "twelve steps" of Alcoholics Anonymous enjoys such popularity and success with all addicts.

On the other hand, many spiritual-religious problems can be solved only with the assistance of psychological knowledge and information that can deal with spiritual immaturity and enhance spiritual growth. For instance, it is helpful to realize the importance of allowing one's emotions to flow freely during prayer. This means that a person needs to be in touch with his or her feelings and not feel guilty about the presence of negative feelings, even during prayer. It also means that prayer is valuable even in the absence of any positive feelings, an absence felt particularly by depressed people. With proper psychological information and understanding, people can avoid unnecessary spiritual obstacles and grow in their spiritual life.

The task of harmonizing the spiritual and the psychological is frequently difficult. One explanation is that many clinicians trained in the behavioral sciences lack knowledge of and formation in the spiritual realm, while those versed in the spiritual often lack sufficient knowledge and understanding of the psychological. At times some in both professions simplistically consider their own approach a panacea for all problems. There can be no spiritual healing without being in touch with the emotional, and no fullness of emotional healing without the spiritual. The human person must be perceived holistically: emotionally, spiritually, and physically.

Psychiatrist Scott Peck in his best seller, *The Road Less Travelled,* has made a significant contribution to integrating the psychological and the spiritual. Also, many moral theologians today have made a further contribution by integrating the spiritual with the psychological as a help to understanding many moral dilemmas.

These two dimensions may be thought of as the psychological and spiritual eyes of the human person, which complement each other. One serves the other in the perception of a total view of life and of oneself. But if one eye is not functioning properly or is closed, it's difficult for one to get a realistic perception of life and an understanding of the human person. If healthy, the two eyes assist us in forming a more holistic view of the person. However, due to the occasional blindness of these eyes, we experience unnecessary human suffering. Psychological blindness results in ignorance about the person; spiritual blindness fosters a profound ignorance in religious areas. It is distressing enough when people lack common sense, but when this is further complicated by religious nonsense it then becomes a case of the blind leading the blind.

In my 27 years as a priest-therapist, I have heard too many stories of needless suffering, *needless* since it was caused by an erroneous understanding of some fundamental emotional or spiritual aspect of the person. At times I have been amazed and alarmed at the breadth and depth of such misunderstanding and at how pervasive it is among people from all walks of life. Hence this book.

The following chapters are a direct result of dealing with such misunderstandings. They treat the basic ideas repeatedly misunderstood by a vast number of people: anger, self-forgiveness, compassion, depression, change, guilt, etc. These concepts seem so common to human functioning, but precisely because of this we can take them for granted. They also seem so basic to our experience that, ironically, we find them difficult to explain and even more difficult to comprehend.

In the Bible (more pertinent for me in the Jesus of the gospels) we find a blending of the human and the spiritual. In fact, the two are often so uniquely interwoven that we are often not even aware of the blending. We find human weakness and failures overcome by spiritual strength, as in the case of a fallen David, who rises because he reaches out to a forgiving God. We see Jesus, who is utterly human and therefore emotional, crying, sad, compassionate, angry, hurting, disappointed, praising, touching, affirming, and affectionate. His feelings are all part of his "spiritual" teaching about hope, love, faith, forgiveness, praying to God as Father, healing, and rising above the material to values of simplicity, mercy, chastity, obedience, love of enemies, peacemaking.

Jesus is the master of spiritual teachings and also the doctor of human behavior. He says, "Follow Me. I am the way, the truth, and the life. I am the light." He calls us to follow him emotionally and spiritually, and very frequently we fail to recognize that his spirituality is part of his humanity.

The aim of *Healing Wounded Emotions: Overcoming Life's*

Hurts is to foster a better understanding, a deeper realization that our human and our spiritual dynamics should complement and be in rhythm with each other as much as our imperfect human condition allows. In all of us there lies a wealth of human and spiritual potential often untapped because of the layers of misunderstanding that obscure it. If this book can show the connection between the two dimensions, and thereby eliminate some of the unnecessary suffering that arises from misunderstanding it, which happens not only to the uneducated but to the educated as well, I shall be content.

God is working in the human condition. But God expects that in our own way we try to cooperate by understanding and using the psychological and spiritual dimensions of our lives. In this way we shall help ourselves work out what God wills for each of us, our sanctification, in a thoroughly human fashion.

1

Problems

Is Anyone Exempt?

We all have problems. They may differ with regard to number, variety, and intensity, but if we are living in this world, then we share this common inheritance and experience.

What's the difference among us when it comes to problems? Simply, some people are troubled and overwhelmed by their problems while others cope and manage them. Often some people handle their problems so well that they are mistakenly judged not to have problems.

One of the primary goals of any counselling and psychotherapy is to help troubled individuals, marriages, and families to help themselves. This means that they are to acknowledge and get in touch with their problems, begin to deal with them and examine the alternative actions to be taken, make a decision and follow through—to go on with life.

Usually within the individual, marriage, or family system, there has been a breakdown in functioning and some corrective action should be considered. Confusion and loss of confidence undermine the built-in potential for healing and functioning. People are overwhelmed by their problems, lose control of themselves and are controlled by the problems. With the loss of control, they begin to feel helpless and hopeless. Anxiety and depression set in, further blocking sound reasoning. They begin to panic and seek immediate and rapid solutions. There are none, of course, and they thus despair.

Human beings are ingenious at devising all kinds of methods to avoid or escape problems. Occasionally we push our problems aside, which is sometimes necessary, but when that becomes the rule rather than the exception, we are headed for trouble. People, otherwise quite rational, make irrational decisions at such times, usually compounding one bad decision with another. Negative thinking and feelings dominate and we act in an irrational and distorted manner. We consider such behavior neurotic.

In many of these situations problems intensify into deeper personal troubles, often because there were warning signs that were not heeded. For example, individuals experiencing unhappiness with themselves and with life in general may blame others, suffer depression and psychosomatic ailments like frequent headaches, ulcers, and chest pains, reflecting that these persons are not handling the stresses in their lives. We may notice husbands and wives, restless in their marriage because of marital dissatisfaction, looking toward other people or becoming overinvolved in other causes, even holy and wholesome ones. Children who act up in school or do not relate to their peers or are withdrawn or rebellious reflect not only their own troubles but those of their family as well, which may be subtle, covert, or denied.

So the difference between those who cope and those who do not will often be the difference between those who face their problems and those who do not. When we avoid problems, they will usually end up controlling and overwhelming us, sooner or later. When we face our problems, we come to grips with reality, and reality, no matter how harsh and painful, keeps us mentally, emotionally, and spiritually sound.

Of course, it is always important to remember that pain is part of the process of growth. As Alcoholics Anonymous says, "No pain, no gain." Whether physical or psychological, pain is really positive because it indicates that something is wrong, something needs to change, a problem needs treatment. If we failed to experience pain, we would lack a system to detect problems. We would not be challenged to change and we would rot.

Because we all have problems, we all have anxiety, depression, and frustration. But are we handling them and in control of them at least most of the time, or are they controlling us most of the time?

It is the same with our insecurities. No one is fully secure. We may have temporary periods of stability, but that's frequently disturbed as we search for another level of stability. Our insecurity helps us to realize our finiteness and the limitations of this world. It forces us to contemplate, beyond the limited realm of human security, a lasting place of security we Christians call heaven, where final peace and security reign with God.

But recognizing and relating to our insecurities help us to know ourselves and stimulate us to further growth. Insecurity and uncertainty are part of our normal existence; we cannot escape them. What counts is how we deal with them and manage to develop and mature through them. Since life is a dynamic process, our grappling with insecurity generates new life within us; not to do so is to stagnate, regress, and become troubled.

In Jesus' parable of the talents, the master gave five to one servant, three to another, and one to the third. Later, when he returned from a journey, he demanded an accounting. The servant who had five gained another five; the one with three increased his to three more; but the servant with one talent buried his and gave the master only the one because he was afraid of losing it. The master praised the first two servants, but he rebuked the third for not earning more. When we fear to face life, we stand the chance of losing it.

If insecurity controls us, we run from life, avoiding risks and refusing to be involved with people; we take no responsibility out of fear or failure. The result is that we become more inadequate, losing our self-confidence as well as self-respect.

In all our problems it is always important to be aware of God's presence within us. We should not, with an immature and infantile religious attitude, presume that God will miraculously remove our problems, but we should rather recognize that God leads us through them, supporting and strengthening us on the way. We should also keep in mind that God brings good out of evil, that confidence in God engenders confidence in ourselves to deal with our difficulties, that God has endowed us with the potential to manage our lives if only we use it. Our insecurity can be either the stimulant to activate our potential, or a deterrent because we refuse to respond to it.

Christ became human not to take away our problems but to teach us to cope with them and so live more responsibly. This is the rich spiritual dimension that we inherit. When we grasp this clearly, we find a deeper meaning in our lives and in our problems, and we can be more in control of our destiny and salvation.

In conclusion, one fact becomes increasingly more evident to me after my years of counseling troubled people: those having a sound and mature faith have an additional support system to cope with their problems; they use not only their human potential but their spiritual as well.

Sometimes we tend to neglect that spiritual dimension. When we do, we short-change ourselves. Frequently, sorry to say, religious ignorance or neurotic religious views sabotage our spiritual powers. Instead of bringing healing, religion brings distortions aggravating our problems.

A strong criticism I have of many psychiatrists, psychologists, and counselors today is their neglect or even denial of that spiritual dimension, especially if it is a concern to the client. I hope more professionals are beginning to acknowledge and encourage the spiritual aspect of their clients. Indeed, we all have problems, but a living faith can make a difference in managing them.

2

Religion

PEACE OR TURMOIL?

Religion is supposed to bring peace, joy, hope, comfort, consolation. It is supposed to help alleviate life's misery, not add to it. Why then do so many suffer torment, turmoil, agony, anxiety, and senseless guilt about their religion? Why do religious people experience misery from religion? Didn't Christ condemn the Pharisees for loading greater burdens on people in the name of religion? Is that what we do to ourselves in the name of religion? Why do we have so many negative attitudes, so much fear of God? That's not religion according to the mind of Jesus. He came to eradicate that kind of religion.

Something is wrong somewhere! Religion doesn't always have answers, but it can give meaning to many of life's problems, sufferings, and dilemmas. It can strengthen us to cope with them. As priest, confessor, and counselor, I am saddened that so many people are tormented in the name of religion. When religion compounds our normally frustrating human situation, it loses its credibility.

Much of this agony is based on misunderstandings, misinterpretations held over from childhood, and misperceptions never

9

clarified—all fortified by years of erroneous thinking. Distorted images and notions of God are not only theologically unsound but can lead to neurosis. The pervasive ignorance and infantile concepts that some people have about God are mind-boggling. And they call it religion!

Senseless religious fears, anxieties, and superstitions make religion look ridiculous. A reasonable God, who gives us reason, appears unreasonable. No wonder reasonable people reject this image. Even in our day some people feel guilty about being happy! Or think that humility means considering oneself worthless. And how about the many who feel that God is out to "get" them? Whenever something goes wrong, they deduce that God is punishing them. It is like the Italian idea of *mal occhio* (the evil eye). When prayers are not answered, some feel that God is angry with them. So why pray?

God doesn't punish us, we punish ourselves. Nor does God condemn us; we condemn ourselves. God is for us—not against us.

There is a great amount of neurotic, un-Christian guilt that saturates people's lives. It is as though Christ's unconditional love and constant forgiveness were never preached. The tragedy here is that some refuse to forgive themselves even after God has forgiven them. That's not religion, that's masochism! It's certainly not Christianity!

We must dig into the deep recesses of our religious thinking and expose these distortions that are so debilitating to genuine faith. We need to confront them in ourselves and in others; they are the demons that Jesus expelled. Such ideas are not only bad religion but contribute to poor mental health.

Often the last vestiges of ignorance that people relinquish are those concerning religion. It often seems safer to remain in ignorance, professing a religion of their childhood, than to risk a deeper growth in faith and trust of God.

Jesus says something different. "Have confidence, don't worry!" "Look at the birds of the air, the lilies of the field; your heavenly Father takes care of them; so he will take care of you." He says we should call God "Father."

Forgiveness is what the message and mission of Jesus are all about. To the adulterous woman Jesus said, "Has no one condemned you? Then neither do I." With his last words, he made an attempt to reach us: "Father, forgive them for they do not know what they are doing."

We have to integrate genuine religious faith in Jesus into our lives. It should work for us, not against us. We must make the transition from an erroneous religious faith to a sound one, from a childish religious faith to an adult; from an immature to a mature. St. Paul's words must be ours, "When I was a child, I used to talk as a child, and think like a child, and argue like a child, but now that I'm an adult, all childish ways are put behind me."

When some professionals, especially those of the clinical persuasion, say to me, "Look what harm religion has done to people," I reply, "You're right, but that's neurotic religion." Often that is the only form of religion these professionals have come to know; they learned it from the distorted views of their clients.

Healthy religion is such a strong support to good mental health and emotional soundness. Over the years, I've seen the difference that Jesus' teaching can make in the lives of the distraught, the hopeless, and the fearful. Jesus heals, but we must have faith in Jesus!

There are three important lessons Jesus teaches us: God always loves us, God always forgives us, God is always present with us. Religion is supposed to bring us peace, joy, hope, comfort, and consolation. If it doesn't, then something is wrong with us—not with our religion or faith.

3

Religion, Psychology

COMPATIBLE?

There are no real contradictions between the principles of sound religion and those of sound psychology. There are at times only apparent ones, the result usually of some misunderstanding. Sound religion and sound psychology support and enhance each other. We should not separate them, but integrate them; not perceive them as mutually exclusive, but as complementary.

Historically, fear and suspicion have sometimes existed between practitioners of psychology and those of religion. This has caused many unnecessary problems. The late Bishop Sheen was the first Catholic authority in both fields to dispel the myth of opposition between them. Still, practitioners in both fields often have been and still are wary of each other.

Psychology and religion should challenge each other. Psychology can clarify Christ's teaching, while deepening and purifying our own spiritual development, and Christ's message can motivate and strengthen good human behavior. Christ's gospel adds another dimension to the meaning of life, a vision beyond the human, on which his gospel is based.

13

In my years as a therapist and counselor, one important fact has emerged from reading the gospels: Christ is the master psychologist; he said it all a long time ago. Succinctly, simply, and superbly, Jesus understands people in their human situation. The more I read the gospels, the more I perceive all the best psychological dynamics at work.

The science of human behavior, with all its wealth of insights, assists us in exploring and analyzing the meaning and depth of Jesus' message. Teaching on both the emotional and spiritual planes, Jesus shows that the two planes coalesce. Perhaps that's why some therapists fail or fall short in the treatment of their clients; they avoid exploring the religious dimension of their clients. On the other hand, the religious minister often shortchanges people by not recognizing the psychological aspects of their lives. In separating the human from the spiritual, we are not seeing the whole person. Isn't lack of wholeness, the alienation within, what mental and emotional illness is all about?

In the gospels Jesus meets people as they are and attempts to raise them up. He relates to both their human and spiritual dimensions. He makes people whole by reconciling the two. In other words, he heals. Consider the paralytic, or Mary Magdalene, or the woman at the well.

As a science, psychology helps us to understand ourselves; religion illuminates our concept of God. Psychology explains the interactions at work in human relationships; religion emphasizes our relationship with God and with one another. Through psychology we get in touch with ourselves; through religion we get in touch with God. If we can't experience ourselves whom we see, how can we experience a God whom we can't see?

Love of God and your neighbor is the cornerstone of Christ's teaching. If I don't love myself, how can I love others and God? Psychology teaches us much about loving, about pitfalls in loving, about real and imagined love, about the demands of love. Believing, accepting, and trusting God requires believing, accepting, and trusting ourselves. With the help of psychology we can root out the contradictions, superficiality, and neurotic dimensions of our personal faith. Over the years we have grown more aware that the influence of psychology has fortified and embellished religious belief and moral thinking.

Psychology teaches us healthy behavior, emotional wholeness, and maturing growth, and how we can rise above and beyond ourselves; Christianity teaches us about redemption, reconciliation, and resurrection. The two, wholly compatible, meet in the human person, supporting and complementing each other. Psychological and religious insight counteract the debilitating forces within and around us, helping us to cope better with life and enrich it. But religion goes beyond this by addressing the faith dimension which rises out of and beyond the human. Jesus always started with the human situation, and St. Thomas Aquinas reminded us that grace builds on nature. The spiritual and emotional are not independent realities in our lives.

Psychological insight is the precious gift by which we can begin to understand ourselves. It doesn't come easily, but it can be facilitated by psychological knowledge. After clients have resolved emotional problems through insight, they are not only free to grow emotionally, but religiously as well. God works through human means to help us develop insight into our behavior.

The more we understand the human dimension of life, the better we can integrate Christ's teaching into our lives. Actually, psychology challenges us to be more responsible because we have achieved insight into our true selves. We can't hide behind platitudes any more or camouflage what we must change in ourselves. The demands of the gospel become more graphic and real. Our sins, which are symptoms of our immaturity, are forgiven, but repentance and reform are still needed. But this is possible only with psychological insight.

Psychology is not a religion, although some regard it as such, but a means to strengthen our understanding of ourselves.

One school of psychological thinking stands above the rest: Viktor Frankl's logotherapy, or therapy through the search for meaning in life. This is beautifully explained in his book, *Man's Search for Meaning.* Our understanding of life and suffering, he argues, depends on the meaning we find in them. "If there is a why, then we can find a how." His writings are a threshold to the gospel.

Jesus gives meaning to suffering and death, to our life as a whole. He has provided us not so much with answers as meaning. The real mental and emotional sickness many suffer from today is not neurosis or psychosis but meaninglessness. People don't know what the meaning of their life is; they wander aimlessly. Jesus knew precisely who he was and what meaning his life had: "I am the light of the world; anyone who follows me will not walk in the dark." "I am the way, the truth and the life." "I am the resurrection. If anyone believes in me, even though he dies, he will live, and whoever believes in me will never die."

Psychology can serve to foster a deeper understanding of ourselves, which will enable us to better follow Jesus. So we should not fear psychology, but hear it out. The Greek philosophers advised, "Know yourself." Freud said, "Be yourself." Christ taught this and much more, "Love yourself."

4

"God's Will"

OR IS IT?

One of the most frequently misused religious state-ments has to be "It's the will of God." Like the aspirin, this state-ment is supposed to serve as a panacea for all of those ailments and misfortunes for which there seems to be no explanation. "It's God's will" has become a religious cliche. Sometimes its use seems like a denial of reality. God, I am afraid, is sometimes short-changed by being blamed for all the ills that befall us. The God of "It's God's will" appears to be insensitive, irrational, cruel, and careless about human affairs. Sometimes "It's God's will" may be used as a cop-out, as when we dodge asking difficult but honest questions about life, or when we avoid searching for the deeper meaning of what has happened to us. Perhaps we just don't want to feel the real pain of it all, or even face the responsibility of our own actions.

I've heard this expression used to explain events ranging from the calamitous to the less important, from a fire that kills a whole family to the death of the family dog. I wish it were all that clear! "It's God's will" is a sacred and meaningful state-ment, but only if properly understood.

17

St. Paul said, "This is the will of God, your sanctification."
God wants us to be saved and to be holy. How does God ac-
complish this? You might answer, through prayer, the Eucharist,
and the other sacraments. Yes, but God also sanctifies us mainly
through the sacrament of living—not just existing. There is a
difference! When we are involved in life, we are living. When
we are passively observing it from the sidelines, so to speak,
we are existing. Sanctification involves entering fully into life.

When we do this, of course, we become enmeshed with
the perennial problem of evil—and God. If God is good, then
why is there evil? Without becoming embroiled in this
philosophical and theological debate, let's realize God wants and
wills good, but only allows evil. God allows it in the sense that
God does not interfere with our freedom to act badly, or control us as if we were puppets. It's the risk God took when he
created us free to do good or evil and free, above all, to love
him. Love cannot be coerced.

When evil appears in our lives—sickness, failure, disappointments, sin—we are disturbed. We ask, "Where is God?
God's supposed to help me." Or when tragedies occur beyond
our control—the senseless death of a friend in an accident, or
a child dying from a rare disease, or the old woman ruthlessly
mugged, or the cancer victim, or a divorce, or any of the endless
list of injustices perpetrated on men and women—we can doubt
not only the presence of a caring God but, if we acknowledge
God exists, a sense of fairness and, yes, reason.

But the person of faith believes God is always with us. St.
Paul tells us that God brings good out of evil. In his own way,
God is always at work, biding his time and slowly weaving the
tapestry of salvation in his world. But, practically speaking, God
wills that we cope with the evil that befalls us. God did not will
that car accident, for which I had no responsibility, but he does
want me to face and use this evil with all its pain-filled and
frustrating ramifications for my own good, as well as for my
growth and sanctification.

In the face of tragedy and the self-evident things to be done, people exercise all sorts of mental gymnastics to discern "the will of God." This seems to be a form of avoidance, a denial of the obvious, a refusal to accept the reality of what is happening. Whatever happens to us—good or evil—God asks that we face it, whether it is just or unjust, logical or illogical, reasonable or unreasonable. It doesn't mean condoning the evil but facing it and possibly changing it.

Divorce is an emotional tragedy that God doesn't will or cause. But if it happens, God does want people to face the reality, not let it destroy them, to work through it and become better people in spite of it. After all has been done to prevent it, the final act is to accept the inevitable and go on living. People die; so do some marriages.

God's will is somewhere in the reality before us yesterday, today, tomorrow. That reality is not vague, but that is where the will of God is. One thing is obvious, that we do what we can to put things right and get on with life. What befalls us is not always right and just, but the death of Christ was not right and just either, but it brought salvation. Christ leaves us a message and an example: "Father, if it is possible, let this cup pass from me, but not my will but yours be done."

Sometimes reality may be the confusion and distress we find in our lives. God's will is that we face this and attempt to work through it. This is what therapy attempts to do, help us to face and cope with the unpleasant realities of our lives, doing the best we can with our limited resources; it means, indeed, picking up our cross. Our destiny is not a plan handed to us, or a passive fatalistic accident, but an active participation in the liturgy of our lives. "Do this in memory of me."

God's will is that we grapple with the uncertainties, the ambiguities and frustrations of daily living. It is not necessarily a clear direction so much as the stark reality of the here and now to be lived. Even the reality of our sins and mistakes produces consequences that are also new realities to be faced and accepted.

In other words, God's final question to us is not, "Did you succeed?" but, "Did you face the realities of your lives?" Indeed, isn't this the continual as well as the final judgment we make on ourselves? One unfortunate aspect of our times is that people avoid reality, and the farther they move from it, the more confused and unhappy they become.

How does all this relate to mental health? Interestingly enough, one of the basic criteria for evaluating a person's mental-emotional health is whether the person is in contact with reality, and if so, how does he or she deal with it? The more we are in touch with reality and cope with it, no matter how painful it may be, the better mental and emotional well being we enjoy, the deeper our sense of healthy self-esteem.

There is, then, a vital and relevant relationship between God's will, reality, and our mental health. God's will on a day-to-day basis is usually not a mystery. It is always before us. It becomes a mystery when we refuse to accept and face reality.

"This is the will of God, your sanctification." We are sanctified through the realities of our life; this is how we work out our salvation. This attitude is not only what gives meaning to the task at hand, but this is what the spiritual life is all about, facing the realities of this life with the mind, spirit, and attitude of Christ. Jesus said, "I have come to do the will of him who sent me." He was a realist, and he teaches us how to face reality and so transcend who we are and the world around us.

We have all known people who were considered very religious and spiritual, but who showed intractable resistance and stubborness in accepting and facing the realities of their lives, which they failed to perceive as God's will. One must question the genuineness of such spirituality.

Jesus never speculated about the problem of evil, but once, very practically, in the parable of the weeds and the wheat, he indicated how to handle this problem. When the steward discovered that someone had sown weeds among the wheat, he cautioned the servant not to pull out the weeds lest the wheat also be destroyed. "Let them both grow together." Jesus shows us something about evil: we must face it and deal with it, but not allow it to overcome us.

This chapter is not an attempt to give answers and explana-

tions for all the madness, tragedies, and injustices in this world—
that's beyond its scope and clearly impossible—but to reaffirm
that God's will for us, as people of faith, is to face and deal with
the day-to-day reality of our lives.

5

Anger

VIRTUE or VICE?

One emotion we were probably never taught to understand or deal with is anger. Because we're not sure how to deal with it, it can very often paralyze our development. It can control us and fill us with anxiety and much unhealthy guilt. So we tend to view it in a negative way, and thus try to avoid it or block it out at all costs. As long as we do this, we remain emotionally immature, stunt our growth, and create unnecessary problems for ourselves. We are never going to be fully human until we are able to deal with anger.

Anger is absolutely necessary for maturity and for healthy human relationships. It is basically a good emotion, and not necessarily sinful. It can be and should be seen as a virtue, if we express and deal with it appropriately.

Anger is an issue for every client I deal with, and very often the underlying cause of many emotional, mental, physical, and relational problems, because it's not properly understood and used. Frequently, we don't recognize it and therefore it goes unexamined and untreated. It is an unresolved issue in every marriage or family relationship where there are problems. It appears even in our relationship with God.

Here are some examples of unhealthy forms of anger: Tom, an educated man, has recently been quite angry with people in his life, especially with people in his office. He has not been able to deal with that anger. He has been so depressed he had to be hospitalized. Betty, a very depressed person, can't get over the loss of her husband who died suddenly. She can't come to grips with it and admit that she's truly angry, especially at God. There's the San Diego mass murderer, who fatally shot 22 people at a McDonald's restaurant. He was a tremendously angry person. There are Jane and Peter, whose marriage is dying. They have no sexual relationship because there's much resentment buried in both of them. There's Sarah, the twelve-year-old, who is having all sorts of headaches and stomach problems because she's very angry at her mother, but her mother doesn't realize it because Sarah does not express the anger. There's Joel, with his anxieties and chest pains, who is very angry at his wife, his son, and his boss, but doesn't know what to do with that anger, and so keeps it hidden, all the while being irritable and unpleasant with the people in his life.

It's important that we develop a positive attitude toward anger we might feel, and above all, that we recognize and admit our anger. If we recognize it we can also possibly recognize the anger that is in others. If we accept our anger along with all our other emotions, we shall see our anger as another aspect of our humanness.

We should feel our anger, deal with it, and reveal it. We should be aware of it, comfortable with it, and allow it. We should ask, "What am I angry about? With whom am I angry?" We should be able to distinguish "logical" anger from "illogical" anger, reasonable from unreasonable anger. Finally, we should reveal it appropriately: express it at the proper time, in the proper place, and in an appropriate manner.

We must take responsibility for the fact that we are angry and for the consequences of our anger. That is, we own our anger! We should not be ashamed of being or feeling angry. In this way we can be in control of it.

It's interesting how the Scriptures deal with the concept and experience of anger. In the Bible, God is often described as "angry." If we read the psalms, which are examples of therapeutic prayer, that is, of really letting out one's feelings, the psalmist prays from his heart, not from his head, and we find plenty of anger. Psalm 38: "O Lord, in your anger punish me not." Psalm 90: "We too are burnt up by your anger and terrified by your fury." Says Jeremiah: "The anger of the Lord shall not abate until he has done and fulfilled what he has determined in his heart." In the book of Numbers, God is described on many occasions as being "angry with the Chosen People" because of their sins and unfaithfulness.

Jesus was angry at times with the scribes and Pharisees and his own disciples and expressed his anger. He attacked the scribes and the Pharisees, "Woe to you, scribes and Pharisees, you frauds. Blind fools!" He's angry and he makes no bones about letting them know. Once Jesus was quite disgusted and angry and didn't mince any words with Peter, "Get behind me, Satan!" We might feel uneasy with an angry Jesus, but he was human, and a part of being human is coming to grips with our anger.

When is anger wrong, destructive, immature, or sinful? When we talk about problematic anger, we are not talking about appropriate anger, which is healthy, but about the two extremes which involve either overreacting or underreacting, either of which is inappropriate.

When we underreact, we repress or suppress our anger, quite unconsciously—we don't realize we're doing it. To repress our anger is one of the most dangerous things we can do to ourselves. It's important to realize that insofar as we repress our anger, we are behaving dishonestly. First of all, we are not being honest with ourselves nor with the people with whom we are dealing. Or we suppress our anger—we are a little more conscious of it, but we choose to block it out, deny it, not let it surface. Again we are dishonest. "Oh, I'm not angry," I say, as I smile and grind my teeth. Or we may "intellectualize" or rationalize our anger away. Yet it's there, inside of us. This repressing and suppressing of angry feelings is the thread that's woven through much emotional, mental, spiritual, and relational problems.

When we overreact, our anger is out of control. It is expressed in temper, rage, fury, which can lead to violence. You find this overreaction in the person who is always angry or agitated. He or she acts in an ugly, obnoxious way.

Underreacting and overreacting are the two extremes of anger we want to avoid, the two ways of expressing anger that are destructive and possibly sinful.

We fear anger. And because we fear it, we suppress it. We fear overreacting because then our anger will control us. Likewise, we also feel guilty about either form of inappropriate anger, which is unhealthy. We are not in control of our lives as long as our anger is not perceived for what it is. We can have overreactive feelings to the point of feeling even murderous, but that is not wrong. Our behavior is what is wrong, not our feelings.

If hidden anger is not brought to the surface and dealt with, it will reappear in some other form. It often appears as a psychological, physical, or psychosomatic problem. People often talk about their physical ailments—colitis, chest pains, hair loss, headaches, ulcers—but the real problem may be the anger they haven't dealt with, anger that has been suppressed, repressed, avoided. And it's going to reappear. It's like a law of physics: if we push something down, it's going to come up in some other form or place. Ordinary depression in most cases is anger turned inward. One major accompanying cause of some mental disorders involving a break with life and reality is unrecognized anger or anger not addressed.

Neglected anger affects us spiritually, too. We feel spiritually dry or are weighed down by the uselessness and the meaninglessness of life. We feel distant from God.

Not dealing with anger can lead to violence and outbursts

of rage. We often say about someone, otherwise apparently calm who acts in a bizarre manner, "He's gone mad." Some people are very controlled, never show anger, and are held up as models. They "never become angry." In such people we usually find a build-up of anger and other unresolved feelings buried within the person that burst forth in bizarre behavior.

Often you can see in these people the signs of undealt-with anger. You see the signs: overreaction to trivial stimuli, violent outbursts, things smashed and thrown, fists through walls.

When we repress or suppress our anger, we're eventually going to overreact and explode, as we do, for example, when a child comes late again to supper, a trifling thing. What we should have done was tell the child we were angry and why we were angry well before this incident took place. Then our justified anger would have been expressed in an appropriate way.

An anger cycle may go like this: you say to yourself after the explosion, "Look what a fool I've made of myself! I won't get angry again." So you go back to stuffing your anger away again. Then, back to overreaction. It is a destructive pattern. Anxiety follows these outbursts, anxiety caused by a sense of loss of self-esteem, of self-worth, and by the presence of guilt.

Many criminals and people with character disorders are really angry people. They're angry about things that happened to them, perhaps especially in their childhood. Now they're taking it out on society. They never resolved their childhood anger and, indeed, they are people who won't even admit that they are angry, but they certainly act angrily.

It is important to recognize the difference between the "state" of anger, and being "an angry person." It's all right to be angry and get over it, to let go of it. But we don't want to be in a state of anger in which we're recognized as permanently angry persons. A constantly angry person is controlled by many unresolved conflicts from the past, or even in the present. They are constantly angry about many unresolved aspects of their lives.

If we do not deal with the anger that we feel, our relationships lead to resentment, bitterness, and hostility. You can see this in problem families and in troubled marriages. In the latter, the anger is frequently connected with extra-marital affairs. A large percent of extra-marital affairs have some element of anger in them. At first those involved may deny any anger, but eventually the anger is recognized on closer examination.

Besides outbursts, anger can also be expressed by silence or coldness. It's one of the cruelest ways of "getting back at" one's spouse or someone close to you. The emotional abuse in this area is much more common than the physical abuse that people suffer in family and marriage relationships.

Again, because people don't manifest their anger in a healthy and appropriate way, misinterpretations take place. For instance, if I do something to you and you're angry at me but don't tell me, I interpret that to mean that you agree with me. I don't know that underneath you're harboring angry feelings, that you really disagree with me. I don't know that you're being dishonest with me. This is destructive.

We may look at the Joneses down the street who come flying out of the front door beating one another up. The whole family's in it, and the police come to separate them. And we say, "Look at the Joneses. They're at it again. I'm glad we're not like them." Well, yes, the Joneses' anger is out of control. But what about the family next door? They get just as angry as the Joneses, but their anger is kept in, unexpressed, with who knows what long-term results. The amount of destructiveness and agony that occurs in people's lives because anger is not recognized and appropriately dealt with is beyond our comprehension. And in some way, the Joneses may be more honest with one another than their neighbors.

Anger is absolutely necessary for mature human relationships! The more intimate I am with you, the more necessary it is for us to be open with each other. And this will sometimes mean showing our anger with each other. But we are afraid of doing this. Why? Because we feel we shall hurt each other. But if we are to be honest with each other, we are going to hurt each other. This is axiomatic in healthy relationships.

There's a distinction, though, between inappropriate hones-ty and appropriate honesty. "Why, you lug-head! How come you're here late? You don't have a brain in your head!" That's inappropriate honesty! That's anger coming out in an un-necessarily hurtful way. But I can also say, "I'm angry with you because this is the third time you've kept me waiting this week." Maybe the other person is hurt, but that's acceptable because I've expressed my anger in a healthy, non-insulting way. Such honest hurt can't be avoided in healthy, close relationships.

Often I don't express my anger because I'm afraid someone "won't like me" or "won't love me." That's insecurity speaking. Or I might be afraid of rupturing a friendship. But what friend-ship is there? If we don't express our angry feelings openly to a friend, then we'll probably talk behind the person's back, or be cold to that person. A relationship that descends to this is not a good one to begin with.

Perhaps we don't show our anger because we are afraid of the anger that will be directed back at us. If we fear another's anger, we can be intimidated and controlled by that person. That's not healthy for a relationship. Parents may be afraid of their children's anger. Or one spouse is afraid of the other's angry reaction and so remains silent and "gives in" in order to avoid the other's anger. This reflects a parent-child relationship rather than a husband-wife relationship. If I'm not comfortable with my own anger, I'm not going to be very comfortable with some-one else's.

My uneasiness with my own anger may come out, inap-propriately, as a laugh. Did you ever see people who should be angry, but laugh instead? They are uncomfortable with the situation and don't know how to deal with it. So they laugh ner-vously and walk away. Consider: when we're angry, do we laugh because we don't know how to handle it? Also, when we're not comfortable with our own anger it means we don't trust ourselves, which in turn means we can't trust ourselves in relationships with other people. And we're not free to the extent that we are controlled by that fear of the anger inside us.

Frequently, people don't express their anger because the

result may be conflict, and God knows, we don't want conflict! And yet, conflict is a necessary, very healthy aspect of any human relationship.

More marriages and families today are dying from silence than from violence. In nine out of ten marriages or families I deal with, this is the situation. Silence. Repressed anger. Unexpressed hostility. Coldness. All are devious and unhealthy ways by which people get back at each other. Every once in a while, though, members of a family begin to yell and scream at each other. It's a nice change of pace. Sometimes I have to get up in the center of my office and hold my hands up like a traffic cop. But I consider that family's behavior healthier than that of the family who keeps it all in. In this situation, at least, people know what the others think and feel.

Anger is very often confused with conflict or violence, but they are not synonymous. Anger doesn't mean violence. It's just anger. Violence is anger out of control. Today, the media often focus on family violence in America. This focusing can work against what therapists are trying to say: that the expression of anger is important and healthy and we have to learn how to deal with it. But the media, because they're not following through with appropriate explanations, are leading people to think they have to bury their anger. I believe that if the media treat this area of behavior, they should do so in depth, and not compound the problem by confusing anger with violence, leading people unwittingly to fear anger when they intend to warn against violence. Sometimes appropriate anger will cause conflict. However, *fair* conflict cannot be avoided in healthy relationships.

When we reveal our anger to another, a conflict or problem is often resolved. People may say, "What's the use of telling that person I'm angry? It doesn't help." But it does. There may be no solution right away, but very often, in the revelation, a solution takes place. There's a clarification of positions; each knows where the other stands; the message gets through; people become more sensitive to each other. For example, a father who tells his son, "Take out the garbage." Thirty minutes later he says it again. An hour later he says, "Damn it, Johnny, take out the garbage!" Johnny jumps up and takes out the garbage and says, "OK, OK. You don't have to make an issue of it." Johnny probably didn't hear the other two times. Sometimes we have to make sure that a statement also has feeling in it, that it has anger in it. Results follow!

When we show our anger to one another, especially in our closer relationships, we sensitize ourselves to one another. We realize what the other person does or doesn't like, what hurts him or her. When you express anger, I know you are hurt. You mean business; you're not to be taken lightly. Then I have to examine my own behavior, my words and actions. I also know that when you get angry with me, you care. You care to take the time and energy to tell me you're angry about something I said or did. It's an act of concern, an act of love.

On the contrary, when I don't want to show my anger, I may be indifferent: "I don't care about you." We need to say to one another, "I feel angry about what you said (or did)." No long sermon is needed. A simple statement of feeling is all that is needed. If we do this, we learn about our differences. By resolving differences we compromise or learn how to live with them. And it is within the context of our differences that we develop our relationships. The inability to resolve differences causes families to fall apart.

Sometimes we have to give the other person and ourselves time to cool off when we're angry. Each of us has a different cooling system. Some people cool off faster than others. We have to know that about ourselves, but also about others. We can forgive someone when we're hurt and angry, but we have to remember to give ourselves time to forget, to heal, to cool off, because feelings can persist for a long time. Even though expressing our anger toward another can strengthen a relationship, sometimes it may also be the force that terminates a relationship, even a marriage. Sometimes we have to realize that maybe a relationship really wasn't what we thought it was, or that it doesn't even exist any more.

Truly, anger is necessary for healthy communication.

Without it, it's impossible for people to relate. We bring our understanding of how to deal with anger and conflict from our family of origin. Did they become angry? Did they overreact? We shall probably deal with our anger in the same way our parents did. It's wise, then, to reflect on and sift through our family background and see it realistically. We have to see what attitudes toward anger we have inherited. Sometimes we may overreact, or go in the opposite direction, reluctant to face conflict. That's why we have to sift through our family background. We should not blindly imitate our parents or, indeed, go to the other extreme. We should try to find a balance.

Parents should teach their children the difference between appropriate and inappropriate anger, and allow them to express their anger. They should never criticize them for expressing anger, but be shown how to express it. "We don't punch, we don't use this type of language. . . ." In this way children begin to learn the difference between healthy and unhealthy anger. Allowing someone else to be angry doesn't necessarily mean that I agree with that person. Children should have the right to be angry, listen to the anger, and then deal with the anger in an appropriate way.

Anger is a power for good or evil. It can be channeled and used not only for our own mental, physical, emotional and spiritual health and maturity, but also for the improvement and healthier functioning of our personal relationships. Furthermore, it is important to realize that beneath much sexual dysfunction in marital relationships is repressed anger.

This means we should be aware of and in touch with our anger, being comfortable with it without fear or guilt. Even if we feel rage, even if we feel like tearing someone apart, these are only *feelings*. We have to allow ourselves to experience them. We have to learn how to be comfortable with uncomfortableness! We have to allow ourselves to be angry with God, our church, our spouse, our children, our parents—dead or alive. Allow that anger to be there.

We also should be able to deal with the anger within us

and to use our intelligence in so doing. We must give ourselves time to reason and reflect our anger; understanding it, we sift out all the elements of it: the logical from the illogical, the reasonable from the unreasonable. We learn the difference between reaction and overreaction. Immediate reaction to our anger is our goal, when possible. Because of circumstances, we sometimes have to delay our angry reaction; we need to cool off. If we're a hothead, we have to learn how to cool off and then go and express anger in a proper way. We put our anger into perspective: of timing, place, and tone. It helps to vocalize our anger if we're overacting! We might shout it out while we're alone driving the car or taking a walk. We might have to talk about it with a friend and perhaps overreact with that person. We may have to sleep on it, so that the next morning the anger will be more appropriate. *Then* we can go and talk to the person who made us angry.

I asked a young boy how he felt about his home situation: his mother and father separated, an inevitable divorce coming up, his father acting strangely. He said, "Well, I feel angry about it." I asked him what he did with his anger. "I go out and kick a soccer ball." I asked him how he felt after that and he said, "Better." He's finding a way to release his anger, and that's healthy. He's getting control of himself and of the anger that is there.

It is important not to compound feelings of anger with guilt feelings, because when we feel guilty and then suppress our anger, we make the whole situation worse. We *can* without guilt be angry with people we love. We all need to deal with that ambivalence. We try to learn this as children, but the ambivalence often goes unresolved. We can love our parents, but we can also be very angry with them and say, "I hate you." But we have to learn how to do this in loving relationships if we expect to have mature loving relationships. We talk things over with another when we're angry, especially when overreacting, someone who will listen, someone trusted, who understands us. Then we can show anger in a proper way because the talking helped to put the anger in perspective. It helps to sort things out.

When I'm in control, then I'm able to reveal my anger, to express it in the proper way and with effective language. The person we're angry at may not always accept my approach. But the purpose in expressing the anger is *not* to change the other person. It's to let him or her know where we are, and how we feel about him or her. What the other does with that anger is his or her choice. In this way a relationship can be strengthened. That's the way we reach the goal of closer, deeper relationships.

We all overreact, especially parents and teachers. And when we do, we should apologize for overreacting, say, slapping a child, or calling him or her a name. But we do not apologize for *being* angry, and we say, "But I *am* angry because you didn't do your homework (or the dishes, or put away your clothes)." We must never let a child off the hook. There was a real reason for our anger. Apologize for the overreaction, but not for the anger. What a beautiful example we give, and how many of us never had that type of lesson in our own families, background, or training. We should expect that people are going to be hurt when we show appropriate anger. It's normal. It's the ordinary hurt that follows honest anger. We may feel bad, but we should not feel guilty.

Sometimes the cause of our anger isn't really horrendous. If somebody cuts us off at a traffic light, we don't want to pursue that person to express our anger. We may say a few choice words to ourselves, or to somebody else in the car. It's the people who are significant in life who really count. We must not allow anger toward them to rest and subside, because that will destroy our relationship. We can develop a destructive attitude, and resentment and bitterness can deepen it. Close relationships require that we express our anger.

Appropriate anger—we must allow ourselves to feel it, deal with it, and be able to reveal it. That is what it means to take responsibility for our lives. And this is what emotional maturity is all about. And this is why anger is a virtue! Anger is truly an important aspect of our lives. How we use it has a great deal to say about what we are going to become. It helps us to be honest, to be genuine, to live a healthy and vibrant life, to trust, to love, and to be intimate.

6

Forgiving

DOES THAT MEAN FORGETTING?

Many of life's situations and religious dimensions are frequently complicated because of a misunderstanding of a fundamental principle of living: the meaning of forgiveness. It is a necessary part of any worthwhile relationship and, it is essential to the Christian's belief system. Without it there is no Christian life.

Given the fact that we accept this, a problem frequently arises when we fail to understand the difference between forgiving and forgetting. Forgiving the person who hurt us and forgetting what that person did are quite different, but we often wrongly consider the two as the same. We think that if our forgiveness is genuine forgetting should follow immediately. We consequently fall victim to much unnecessary emotional and spiritual conflict. This conflict can cause unhealthy guilt, which further aggravates our uneasy state of mind, and we are at odds with ourselves. Because we know we are willing to forgive but still have those unforgiving negative feelings, we feel hypocritical.

This confusion, a very distressing problem, persists in almost epidemic proportions among believing Christians both young and old, educated and uneducated, traditional and progressive.

What is happening here? People fail to make a very simple but important distinction between forgiveness as an act, and forgiveness as a feeling. If we don't make this distinction, we find ourselves locked into an apparent dilemma.

The act of forgiveness is just that: an act; it's a choice, a decision based on our Christian convictions. It is an act of the will and intellect, based on our reasonableness. It's a reaching out to a person, inviting him or her back into a former relationship. It can be a difficult act but a firm one; it can be cold and devoid of accompanying warm, positive feelings, but nonetheless genuine. I suggest that Christ's act of forgiveness on the cross: "Father, forgive them for they know not what they are doing" might have been of this nature. It's hard to imagine that amid all his physical and emotional agony that Jesus had warm, positive feelings!

The *act* of forgiveness can be a fact but the *feeling* of forgiveness may come only in time. When we confront these "unforgiving feelings," deal with them honestly, and work through them, then they will gradually become dissipated. Then the forgetting process commences. The process of forgetting is just that, a process that involves our feelings, which we must respect and understand. We have no control over how we feel, only over how we act and handle our feelings. Do we allow them to control us or do we control them? They control us when, for example, we act meanly, coldly, or with hostility to another person.

In regard to feelings, people are frequently confused with regard to what is sinful. Sin is not in our feelings but in our behavior. One spouse who has forgiven the other must allow his or her negative feelngs to subside and the warm feelings to return. For even when we forgive, resentful feelings are often still present and this is all right; but if we act in a resentful way, it is sinful.

Resolving negative feelings requires time and effort. How much time and effort may vary, depending on our personality and temperament and on how much we've been hurt. Once we realize, however, that feelings of forgiveness need not be present with each act of forgiveness, we will have freed ourselves of self-contradictory feelings, of self-condemnation and much confusion. We can thus avoid unnecessary guilt and begin to deal with real guilt.

The negative feelings of anger and resentment that result from being hurt are not only normal, but we would be less than human if we did not experience them. Sometimes people deny such feelings because they don't want to deal with them. They feel embarrassed, uncomfortable, and guilty about them. But these feelings are real, although they are not always reasonable. They must be faced and accepted. We need to confront the unreasonable guilt feelings surrounding our temporary inability to forget, lest they aggravate our situation and cause us to feel less worthy.

People often feel hypocritical and guilty because, while they profess to be Christian and they want to forgive, they can't dispel their negative feelings. "If I have forgiven this person, then why am I still bothered with these terrible feelings of hate and resentment? I guess," the person reasons, "I have not truly forgiven."

The truth is that we can genuinely forgive even though time is required to forget and to heal our negative feelings. We have to live with those feelings for a while. The divorced, the victims of crime, injustice, terrorism and war, parents hurt and rejected by their children, children neglected and mistreated by their parents, the old who are overlooked and the young who are not heard—all who suffer the hurts, misunderstandings, and insensitivities of daily living can forgive, but we must realize that forgetting will take time.

We cannot program ourselves into a set time-frame for forgetting. Each one of us has a different, unique healing ability. We have to use all the mental, emotional, and spiritual means to help ourselves heal and forget.

Sometimes people seek special counseling to help them handle, understand, and heal their feelings when they seem to be losing control of their lives.

Some hurts we may never forget; even though wounds may heal, scars often remain. But these scars, like those of Christ, can be signs that we are able, with his help, to forgive as he forgave.

As we give ourselves time to forgive, we should also be ready to give time to those we have offended. Even though they have forgiven us, we must allow them space and time to be affectionate and to trust us again. Often this is not understood enough in married and family life. We grow impatient; we expect a sundered relationship to return to normal immediately. Frequently hurts and subsequent forgiveness can be the basis for strengthening relationships, but at times, sorry to say, some relationships are never the same again.

Another important aspect of this subject is this: forgetting does not necessarily mean forgiving! Without the experience of forgiveness, forgetting can be a way of avoiding dealing with the pain and hurt of being offended. By burying our hurt feelngs we prevent ourselves from truly arriving at forgiveness. Forgetting will never be possible until we first experience and acknowledge a hurt, and then go through the struggle and satisfaction of forgiving. Beware of people who too quickly say, "Forget about it." They leave us hanging, unsure of how they truly feel. We wonder if we are forgiven. When people just forget, they are usually sweeping negative feelings under the rug, and this can be very dangerous. Buried negative feelings will manifest themselves in time and in some negative form.

The act of forgiving is one thing, but the art of forgetting is another; it takes time. It is a human process that can be facilitated by prayer and reflection and perhaps counseling. Like God, we often can forgive immediately, but only God can forget immediately.

7

Self-Forgiveness

IS IT OVERLOOKED?

The word "Christian" is synonymous with forgiveness. Christ reveals not only God's forgiveness of us, and asks that we forgive one another, but also implies that we forgive ourselves. This last aspect of Christ's message is not stressed or discussed enough. However, if we call ourselves Christian, we have to be able to forgive ourselves. If we have not forgiven ourselves, then we have not experienced the fullness of redemption, been reconciled with ourselves, nor achieved Christian maturity.

This statement is strong, even a bit shocking, but it should be taken seriously. People are often stunned when I ask, after they have admitted to a failure or a sin, "You believe God has forgiven you, but have you forgiven yourself?" Many Christians hardly consider this.

Over the years I've become convinced that a great many people accept God's forgiveness on a superficial level. Why? Because the deeper aspect of forgiveness that some of us never experience is self-forgiveness. We believe God has forgiven us; now he invites us to forgive ourselves. How often our response

41

is "I couldn't do that!" No doubt self-forgiveness is difficult and demanding for many. But unless we take God seriously and apply his forgiveness by actually forgiving ourselves, we will never genuinely experience God's forgiveness, the fullness of redemption, or reconciliation with ourselves. We live a contradiction by accepting God's forgiveness but not our own.

This applies not only to people in mental institutions and to criminals and people experiencing emotional problems, not only to those who have committed serious sins, but to ordinary people. Over the years, when I questioned people about self-forgiveness I found a clear reluctance to do so. This was common to young and old, male and female, to lay people, priests, and religious.

Why? Because many seem to have a need to punish themselves after sinning. What better way than by withholding forgiveness? We are not "worthy" of it, so we attack our self-esteem, which causes us to feel worthless. This is a type of masochistic martyrdom, forgetting that God's forgiveness tells us we are worthwhile. "How could we have done such a thing?" we ask. Self-forgiveness, we wrongly think, means condoning what we have done, and so we condemn ourselves—irrationally. Instead of accepting ourselves just the way we are, with all our limitations—as God does—our pride leads us to consider ourselves the way we were or should be.

Often we refuse self-forgiveness because we are disappointed in ourselves. Through self-pity, self-condemnation, or self-punishment, we choose a form of self-centered behavior and end up blocking God's final flood of healing forgiveness and love. The process of a deeper redemption is stymied.

This disappointment is so oppressive that it sends us into a tailspin of continual failure. "So what's the use?" we groan. We give up on ourselves. We refuse to rise up, to pick up our cross of human frailty and follow Jesus.

On the other hand, by forgiving ourselves we can make our sins and failures work for us. We transcend the human situation and gain precious insight into ourselves. We grow through the pain of failure, in addition to reflecting praise and glory to the ceaseless magnitude of God's love.

If we persist in not forgiving ourselves, we build up reserves of stagnant guilt, whether we recognize this fact or not. We become spiritually and emotionally numb, even depressed, and controlled by these worthless feelings. We sink into a quagmire of immobilizing despair. Isn't this unreasonable, illogical, and neurotic? But many otherwise intelligent people insist on following such a pattern. In which case our religious faith is not working for us but against us—and that is tragic. It also makes our religion less credible to the world around us. Forgiving ourselves is difficult; we have to work at it, but we can do it. It is not only the ultimate challenge of Christian redemption and reconciliation, but also the key to mental, emotional, and spiritual health and healing.

We shouldn't be too quick to say that we are not among those who fail to forgive themselves. We have to be very sensitive and honest about the subtle forms this failure can take. Our feelings may not want to let go of unreasonable guilt, but our intellect must dwell on the unconditional love of God for us and proclaim self-forgiveness. When we forgive ourselves, we allow God's forgiveness to come into our lives abundantly. We begin to experience the resurrection now.

The source of many emotional conflicts is the refusal to forgive self. People suffering these emotional conflicts will never heal emotionally or spiritually until they forgive themselves, nor will they ever be able genuinely to forgive their brothers and sisters. "Love God and your neighbor as yourself." Genuine love of self demands self-forgiveness. All mental health professionals should be sensitive to the fact that many of their clients will never heal, find inner peace, or make progress in therapy until they experience self-forgiveness. When that happens, healing and progress become possible.

Of course for this to happen the faith dimension of the individual should be activated and challenged. The pity is that this faith dimension is frequently passed over, and some clinical technique substituted.

Lastly, self-forgiveness doesn't mean absolving ourselves of the responsibilities and consequences of our actions but emphasizes them all the more. It doesn't mean self-pity, but accountability and repentance, and change. It doesn't mean whitewashing or condoning our sins, but facing the harsh realities of our actions and picking up our cross and following Jesus.

We can't really live a full and loving life unless we possess the mature faith that enables us to forgive ourselves, no matter what has "gone wrong" in our lives. Then we can truly let go, let God in, go on living and loving. Self-forgiveness is often the difference between the fully redeemed Christian and the superficially redeemed Christian; between the Christian who has not only been reconciled with God but with self; between the mature Christian and the immature Christian.

8

Guilt

STIMULANT OR TORMENT?

Guilt is a fact of life, and feeling guilty is a normal experience for most of us. When we sin, that is, when we knowingly hurt another or act against our own values or convictions, we should experience guilt, if not emotionally then at least mentally. Scripture says even the just man fails seven times a day. How we handle such guilt feelings makes a difference whether our spiritual and emotional development is healthy or unhealthy.

Only the psychopathic person—the kind of person who mugs an old woman and feels no remorse—claims not to experience any guilt. This type of personality is not the subject of our discussion. Rather we shall discuss those who experience the "ordinary guilts" of life. For people to claim that we should never feel guilty about anything is ridiculous. If this were true, we indeed would have a psychopathic society. None of us would be safe with anyone else. Normal healthy guilt is a protector of society's health.

Guilt can be a stimulant, a quick, painful jolt to incite us to change. Feelings of guilt help us to acknowledge that we have done wrong—and that's good! Coming to grips with sin is a dimension of sanity. If we don't allow them to overwhelm us, feelings of guilt should bring us to seek forgiveness from God, from others, and from ourselves; they should stimulate us to change our ways. Such feelings also should help us learn from our failures. Do we ever stop to realize how much our lives consist of failures, mistakes, sins? The salient questions are: how do we cope with the consequent guilt feelings and how much do we learn from them?

Each failure is an occasion for learning, for gaining valuable insights into ourselves, and for taking more responsibility for our lives. Additionally, for Christians, failure is an opportunity for enhancing our relationship with God by experiencing and increasing our faith in his constant redeeming love. We learn that guilt stimulates us to reaffirm that we are worthwhile and should not be condemned as persons, in spite of our sins. Once again we reflect on Paul's and Augustine's teaching that out of evil God brings good. The Spirit of God is always working in our human frailty.

But we are so often disappointed by our moral failures that our guilt refuses to disappear and we condemn ourselves. In such situations, guilt works against us, rather than for us; it becomes a torment rather than a stimulant. We become less human and thus less Christian; we experience not redemption but rejection. Unlike the psychopath who is imprisoned by others, we imprison ourselves—behind the bars of our guilt.

Holding on to our unresolved guilt is described as "guilt after the fact." It is guilt still lingering, still burdening and immobilizing us after we have sought forgiveness and repented, and even made reparation for actual sin. Guilt that controls us "after the fact" of forgiveness becomes unhealthy, or neurotic guilt, which impedes our normal functioning. Holding on to guilt is a species of self-punishment, or self-imposed martyrdom, of which there is much more in our society than we are aware. It can be so subtle and unconscious that it eludes even the detection of the most perceptive counselor or confessor. Such masochism is not virtuous but a disease detrimental to sound religious growth. It implies a perfectionism that is un-Christian, unrealistic, and, as such, destructive.

We sometimes observe such self-punishment after a marital break-up, the death of a loved one, the loss of a job, or a sudden disappointment; or when someone deliberately hurts another or is mean or vengeful. The guilty party in these cases tortures self needlessly for failing, and refuses to forgive self. Sometimes people consciously or unconsciously do hurtful things to themselves as a way of punishing themselves.

I recall people who admitted having caused their own car accidents to punish themselves. Sometimes people even persist in being nasty to others to prove that they really are rotten — and they drive people away from them, which proves that they are rotten. People even allow others to harm them as a form of deserved punishment; for example, a wife allows herself to be abused. The rationale of this behavior is: "I've done wrong, I'm no good and I deserve to be punished."

There is nothing more powerful in undermining one's self-image and self-esteem than these negative attacks and messages coming from unresolved guilt. It is so important to be in touch with and bring to the surface our subtle and buried guilt — or it will sabotage our lives. Thus it is no great honor to boast that one neither feels nor admits to guilt for real wrong. Such denied guilt will haunt us in other forms: in anxiety, depression, restlessness, or various psychosomatic disorders.

Sometimes we experience guilt feelings for no apparent reason. We are conscious of no deliberate wrong. A person will say, "I feel guilty and I can't say why." Such unreasonable guilt feelings can create endless unrest and torment. From time to time we may be bothered by such feelings. If we allow them to "get" to us they can control our lives. They must instead be confronted with the intelligence God gave us. They are mostly illogical and unfounded. Feeling guilt about missing Mass, or an appointment or celebration, even though we are ill, is an example of this. People have confessed they missed Mass when the weather was terrible. "Oh, I know I don't need to confess it, Father, but I feel better," they say. No reasoning can reach such people. We may rightly feel bad or disappointed about such happenings, but we never should allow ourselves to feel guilty about them or allow such guilt to control us.

Another common problem occurs when we feel guilty for having angry, hateful, murderous, or sexual feelings. Our feelings are not sins; only our behavior may be sinful. We neither condone nor condemn these feelings, but we should try to understand them. Therefore we should allow ourselves to feel these so-called negative feelings but not allow them to determine our behavior. Consequently it is absolutely futile to confess negative and immoral feelings just because we feel guilty about them.

In connection with this, there are times when the intensity of our guilt feelings is out of proportion to the act we have committed. A person who loves rabbits feels overwhelmed with guilt because she killed a rabbit while driving excessively fast down a country road. In such an instance there is need to cultivate a strong, reasonable approach toward the action in order to gain a balanced perspective on our mistakes, feelings, and sins.

Frequently we need to understand our family background when we have particular difficulties concerning unreasonable guilt. We often uncover in our family background an atmosphere and pattern of unhealthy guilt that consciously and unconsciously has been a part of our upbringing. In such a case, we need to resolve this and grow beyond that background.

It also happens that someone makes us feel guilty for some act we were not responsible for. Feeling guilt arising from that source may also be due to our upbringing. We need to take the responsibility for allowing ourselves to feel guilty and then we can deal with the feeling more honestly and effectively. If we allow others to make us feel guilty when we shouldn't, then they can control and manipulate us, knowingly or unknowingly. All this happens in countless different ways in our relationships, especially in marriage and in families. Of course this type of guilt can become quite destructive and destroy our relationships. Making another feel guilty unfairly, without cause, is basically a put-down, and an attempt to destroy another's self-confidence.

This occurs so dramatically today in the case of parents who feel unreasonably guilty about their children's behavior and who are thus controlled by their children. Parents feel guilty for disciplining their children or for being angry with them; they feel guilty when their children fail in school or in life, get into trouble, and sometimes even when the children divorce. Some parents feel guilty when their children are angry with them or hate them. The list is endless and quite disturbing. No wonder so many families are in serious trouble today. The children are controlling the parents by making them feel unreasonable guilt. This sort of guilt can attack the most confident parents if it is not challenged. It is important to remember that some people will dump the responsibility for all their mistakes on anyone who might be guilty enough to allow this to be done.

How often people feel guilty because they have expressed quite appropriate anger and as a result another person has felt hurt? The hurt that comes from facing the truth can't be avoided in day-to-day relating; such hurt is a normal part of living. Our frankness can be painful, but as long as it is appropriate and unmalicious we need not feel guilty about it. Being honest is part of developing a trusting relationship. We truly hurt one another so often because we fail to be honest with each other—and for this we *should* feel guilty. So many marriages and families are hurting due to an avoidance of honesty or a fear of conflict. So many marriages and families are dying because of silence, not violence. In these areas our guilt is often misplaced.

Authentic guilt feelings are to be faced and resolved by seeking forgiveness, by making amends or apologies. False guilt feelings will be resolved or at least controlled by confrontation and understanding. This often works havoc in our lives on account of religious ignorance and misunderstanding. The more I listen to people's problems, the more I become convinced that ignorance and misunderstanding in the religious sphere create many needless troubles. Among those is unresolved and unreasonable guilt, which pervades and controls our lives. Sometimes a penitent's narration of sins is nothing more than a description of the symptoms of neurotic (irrational) guilt. To be freed from such debilitating guilt requires a deeper understanding of God's mercy, further religious education, and clarification of how our emotions work. Professional help should be considered if irrational guilt hinders our daily functioning.

One of the more agonizing problems in this area is called scrupulosity. The scrupulous person constantly feels intensely guilty for alleged, small wrongs or sins. Actions that for most people would be natural or, even if wrong, relatively unimportant, become for scrupulous people monumental.

The scrupulous person will agonize over one or another act, be indecisive, and suffer torments, unable to find peace. There is the constant feeling that he or she has sinned and is obsessed with the consequent guilt.

Scrupulosity is a moral-religious illness that is part of the disease of the obsessive-compulsive personality. It needs to be treated clinically as well as, at times, medically. In the past few years there have been significant advances in the treatment of this illness.

In any case, frequent reception of the sacrament of reconciliation as a cure for the scrupulous person's unhealthy guilt can be futile and may only aggravate the problem. Since he or she has been forgiven but may still feel guilty, the guilt feelings need to be resolved. And if there was no sin in the first place and the person still feels guilty, the irrational guilt must be confronted. In either case, repeating the sacrament is not the answer.

In the gospels Jesus always helps people recognize their guilt by getting them to admit their sins. Look at Zacchaeus, the woman at the well, the woman caught in adultery. He offers them forgiveness, freedom from sin and guilt. He asks that they trust enough in him and the Father to let go of guilt. When we hold on to guilt we jeopardize the redemptive process.

Resolving our guilt doesn't mean releasing us from the consequences of our sins and failures. These we must live with and make reparation for; for example, you must pay for the dish you threw at your brother and broke; you must set the record straight when you lie about someone. Changing our lives (true repentance) and making reparation for our sins are effective means toward resolving our guilt.

A particularly painful reality is that sometimes we hurt another person very deeply and, even though we are sorry and the person forgives us, the consequence may be such that the relationship will never be the same or even may never be again. Such is the regrettable case in a divorce when one partner is unable to persuade the other to take him or her back. In these situations the guilt feelings need much more time to be dissipated.

When we look at some of the multi-faceted complications of guilt, we don't wonder that the modern day world tries to avoid guilt by denying sin. At first this approach appears to be the easier way out, but in the long run it creates deeper emotional and spiritual problems because we deny the reality of the human situation we live in.

Indeed when we live according to the gospels we gradually realize that Jesus uses guilt as a stimulant to growth and change, but not as a means of torment. The torment is our doing.

9

Depression

CAN WE EXPRESS IT?

"Out of the depths, I cry to you, O Lord." The psalmist reflects the agony and emptiness we experience when we are feeling "down," or in the dumps, or depressed. Depression is a human pain all experience occasionally.

Due to medical research we can now diagnose certain states of depression as being physical in origin. A chemical imbalance results in a deep depression which arises neither from situations in the person's life nor from an inability to cope with problems. Once depression is found to have a physical origin it can be treated with specific medications (anti-depressants) which are usually quite effective. It is sad that people will often refuse such medication claiming, mistakenly, that they don't want to be dependent on medicine and want to conquer the depression by themselves. This is as foolish as attempting to wish away diabetes or high blood pressure without the necessary medication.

However, the depression I am speaking about is the ordinary depression that arises from certain life situations: personal loss, disappointment, failure, frustration, fear, etc. At times such

53

depression can be acute due to the seriousness of the situation, such as the sudden death of a loved one or the realization that one has cancer. Then there are those "lows" we feel when we are hurt, misunderstood, have lost a friend or job opportunity, or have simply failed in one way or another.

Ordinary depression is normal, and we all need some time to work through the experience. Depression becomes a problem only when we neglect to deal with it; then it persists and begins to get the better of us. Sometimes this sort of severe depression also requires medication and counselling for a period.

For a man or woman to remain depressed for an extended period after the death of a spouse is such a case. Another example, at the opposite extreme, is the person who becomes and remains deeply depressed over losing the lottery by two numbers. Neither case is normal. In these and other cases we notice that often the object or person lost is like an anchor attached to the depressed person, dragging the person down to the depths, holding him or her there. The problem lies in being unable to accept the inevitable and to let go of the lost object or person, and in the failure to work through the grieving process.

The experience of loss, which is one of the causes of depression, generates a sense of hopelessness, which in turn makes us feel helpless. Often the depressed person becomes immoblized; the ability to function normally is impaired. The level of motivation becomes low, and meaninglessness clouds one's vision of life.

Such stages and causes of depression can overpower and cripple a person and prevent him or her from living effectively. "Ordinary" depression can grow worse and become chronic if it is not resolved.

Depression must be understood if it is to be treated and prevented. It is important to recognize and admit it when it occurs. We should reflect on what may be causing it and then react to the perceived causes. In this way we can prevent depression from disrupting our lives extensively and can utilize it for a better understanding of ourselves and for personal growth.

One of the fundamental and most common causes for depression is repression. Repression takes place when we bury painful and negative feelings—memories, fears, etc.—inside ourselves, resulting in our holding in all types of confused, distorted, and distressing thoughts and feelings. If these are not faced and dealt with but allowed to fester, they cause a build-up of tremendous tensions and inner conflicts which adversely affect our peace of mind and pull us down into depression. Frequently people try to forget unpleasant and unwanted feelings and thoughts or push them aside, but they won't go away until they are faced.

When we repress our negative feelings we feel tired, we suffer a loss of incentive, and we feel apathetic because of the amount of energy these inner conflicts consume and the effort it takes to hold them in. People in this state feel confused and unsure of what they are really thinking and feeling. A period like this is not a time to make major decisions. We should wait until some of this inner turmoil has been resolved, and our thoughts and feelings clarified.

How do we do this? By expression. If repression can cause depression, then expression can begin to alleviate it by forcing to the surface all those tangled and twisted thoughts and feelings that need to see the light of day, to be seen for what they are. We do this by expressing our feelings to someone close to us whom we trust enough to reveal them to, someone who may not agree with us or even always understand us but who is willing to listen carefully and to help us sort things out. I usually ask my clients, "Do you have a close friend with whom you can talk about this, a friend who communicates, who confronts and challenges you?" Depressed people need to talk; they need a friend who will listen and feel with them. But often the depressed person wants to withdraw and thus he or she regresses.

If you have friends who want to do that, don't let them! Encourage and even pressure them to communicate what they are feeling, to get things out of the darkness into the light, out "on the table" where a new and realistic perception of all the repressed material will be possible. The light-bringing Spirit of God works in such a process and healing can begin.

This need for expression may also be satisfied by being in touch with our inner world so that we are aware of our act of repressing and of being controlled by it. Then we can courageously confront the distorted feelings within. We must not allow them to overwhelm us, nor should we believe or trust in them.

We can sort things out better when we verbalize what we feel, when we hear ourselves speaking. The listening process gives us permission to be ourselves. Both the verbalizing and the listening must support each other and continue until we gain control of our depression.

With regard to the dialog with ourselves, prayer may be another source of help, a real "gut-level prayer" for help. Such prayer is prevalent in the psalms. "Out of the depths I cry to you, O Lord. Lord, hear my prayer!" In the darkness when we feel empty and dry, we share our agonies with God in prayer. We let God touch, absorb, and heal our twisted, knotted spirit. In such states our trust in God is tested but it is also in such states that our trust truly expands.

What might we find stuffed away underneath all the depression? There are a number of factors that are repressed, but some of the most significant are: anxieties, anger, and negative thinking. Anxieties are those unreasonable fears about our lives and about the future, which gnaw away at us. Many of these fears are illogical and unreasonable, yet they influence our lives and make us feel insecure and lacking in self-confidence. If we discuss them and view them more openly we can be more in control of them. In a dialog with a trusted friend this result is often possible. Such open and honest communication might not always solve the problems, but it can often resolve the depression. Very often the solution is in the revelation!

The second contributing factor is repressed anger, by far one of the most devastating causes of depression. In fact, the common psychological definition of depression is "anger turned inward." What makes it so dangerous is that very often it is not recognized; it's avoided or denied. As I mentioned in an earlier chapter, we fear anger, and so we create an unnecessary amount of pressure and unresolved conflict within us, and this pulls our spirits downward.

People will usually admit they are hurt by another, disturbed by the loss of a friendship, a job, or the death of a spouse, but they will often not be honest and admit the accompanying anger or deal with it. People must give themselves permission to experience their anger and express it appropriately, when necessary, without guilt.

When the anger has been expressed, shared with another or in some way worked out, the person is free to mobilize energies for positive constructive living instead of wallowing in passive, destructive repression. Sometimes people unconsciously or consciously prefer the helpless depressed state, since it removes the responsibility of grappling with pertinent problems and considering effective decisions.

The third contributing factor to depression is negative thinking, which subtley or obviously controls a person's self-esteem and self-image. When people are in low spirits they tend to be down on themselves. In such a depressive state worthless feelings and ideas multiply; the person becomes his or her own worst enemy through self-condemnation. In these cases we also find much guilt that has not been abandoned and continues to haunt the person.

Therefore we must ferret out all such negative thinking about ourselves if we are to defeat depression. We have to confront the unreasonable statement we are making to ourselves and the often ridiculous conclusions we are drawing: for example, that we are bad or worthless since we have sinned, or hurt another, or failed in school, on the job, or in marriage. We have to convince ourselves that we can recover and have hope for our future, that even though an action was wrong, the person who did it is good.

The refusal to forgive ourselves only consigns us to the torture chambers of our depressed mind, and we become quite self-centered as we celebrate pity for ourselves. All of this constitutes a vicious circle that drags us further into depression. This is not only emotionally destructive, but it can become a situation where even suicide is considered.

Negative thinking is also fueled by perfectionism, which is always unrealistic and destructive. Unrealistic expectations about ourselves and others is continually setting us up for disappointment and further depression.

Some of the depression that people experience after the Christmas holidays is an example of this. The high emotional expectations of what the holidays could have been or should have been; the frantic, harried attempts to make them the "best ever," are all preparing us for a negative reaction. Christmas can become "the great American set-up." Disappointments leave us empty, frustrated, disgusted, disillusioned, and probably angry, so that January and February, already bleak and dismal in many parts of the continent, appear even more gloom-laden than usual. The problems we were wrestling with in November seem almost insurmountable in January. After we fall from such an unrealistic high to new depths, no wonder we contemplate the future with depression.

Depression can best be confronted and checked by realistic thinking, by accepting ourselves and being happy with who we are as we continue to try to become better persons. Here is where the belief about God's unconditional love for us, the story of redemption and God's constant forgiveness can help us emotionally as it also helps us to mature as Christians. Here again we see how Christians may make their faith work for them. So an application of faith can work wonders for the depressed.

In all three of these factors contributing to depression—anxiety, anger, negative thinking—the significant method that will assist us to counteract them is expression.

Lastly, the importance of not losing hope must be stressed. Since depression is so uniquely tied up with a sense of loss, it is also quite easy to lose hope: in ourselves, in others, in God. Without hope we succumb to helplessness, and we may then relinquish the responsibility for our own lives. If we are Christian, then we are people of hope, which sustains us and draws us forward even in the darkness, for God is with us and working with us.

There is no reason to despair. Depression is a treatable disease. It may require medication, but it also needs to be expressed and this expression, combined with hope in God, will lead to healing.

The Bible is the story of God constantly calling his people out of something: out of chaos, out of Egypt, out of captivity, out of darkness, out of the depths, out of trouble. And so he calls us out of depression. But God does not just call us out of something, but into something else, something better. He calls from chaos to creation, from Egypt to the Promised Land, from darkness into his own wonderful light. Depression, then, can be the occasion for moving into a new stage of emotional and spiritual growth. Perhaps someone or something was lost—that cannot be denied—nor can a loss be underestimated or replaced, but something new has been gained, something frequently less tangible but not any less real.

In our bouts of depression we must search for the deeper meaning of what is happening to us. Viktor Frankl writes that if we can find out *why* something happens to us, then we can endure the *how*. For Christians, Christ more than anyone else gives meaning to our existence. But each one must find that meaning. Each time we face a state of depression we are being called to something greater. When we find meaning we sustain our hope; we experience healing and mobilize our lives for a world we may never have realized existed or maybe never wanted to exist. Christ's disciples did not realize that the depression of Good Friday would lead to the joy of an Easter Sunday resurrection.

10

Self-Criticism

OR SELF-CONDEMNATION?

In the story of the adulterous woman (John 8:1-11), Jesus appears not only as a wise defense lawyer, but also as an empathetic psychologist. When the Pharisees arrogantly act as judge and jury of the embarrassed woman, considering themselves impeccable, they demonstrate the tragedy of human beings acting without personal insight into their own lives.

These are some of the more obvious examples: the divorced man who can't see his part in a marital break-up but can only blame his former wife; the student who doesn't understand why she had failing grades; the teenager who blames his parents and family for the way he feels; the alcoholic who doesn't comprehend why she drinks; the emotionally troubled man who is not in touch with his feelings and inner world; the overweight woman using food as an escape and source of consolation; all those depressed people unaware of their buried anger; the so-called lazy people, afraid of failure and lacking self-confidence; the emotionally immature who marry out of their excessive needs and call it love.

As the problems of such people increase, their insight

decreases, or so it seems. Is it any wonder that these people lack insight into themselves or their behavior, easily blaming others for their mistakes, and finding it so difficult to apologize or admit any wrong? It is as if any admission would annihilate them and their self-esteem. There is a basic fear of failure.

Jesus conveys to the Pharisees that they themselves are not without sin. Eventually they get the message; they recognize their own sins and sheepishly disappear. Jesus teaches us not to condemn others before we take a hard critical look at ourselves.

Condemnation by another is difficult enough to hear, but self-condemnation seems to me to be even more difficult to bear, given its destructiveness. In dealing with the adulterous woman, Jesus leaves us an important lesson in loving and living with ourselves in spite of our sins and failures. He says to her, "Woman, has no one condemned you?" "No one, Sir," she replies. Jesus responds, "Then neither do I. Go and sin no more." God does not condemn us even though others may condemn us or we may condemn ourselves. Implicit in this is that Jesus indicates we should be critical of ourselves as he urged the Pharisees to be, but not condemn ourselves.

There's a fine line between self-criticism and self-condemnation, but also a great difference. Because of this, people are afraid to look at themselves critically for fear that they will condemn themselves. They equate the two. I've encountered so many otherwise intelligent and talented people who have no insight into themselves. They don't know themselves, and they dread and reject any professional or even friendly advice to look inward and know themselves. Healthy self-criticism produces insight, and insight helps us to know ourselves, with the subsequent possibility of change and growth.

Self-criticism is absolutely necessary for emotional and spiritual maturity. The amount of insight people have often means the difference between a healthy and sick marriage or family. Self-criticism is positive and constructive. Once we cease fearing it, it can become freeing, exhilarating, and self-satisfying.

It challenges us to accept and love the reality of who we truly are, not the false image of who we wish we were. Thus we limit our unrealistic expectations and the consequent useless frustrations we bring upon ourselves. Healthy self-criticism challenges us to greater heights of human and Christian development. The better we can read ourselves, the more we can know and understand others, as well as be sensitive to their needs.

Self-criticism is based on the understanding that we are good and worthwhile, that we can become better, that we can learn from our failures and grow, that without failure we cannot change or know ourselves and our limitations. The paradox is that in failure, which is a part of life, we change. The crucial question is how we handle and react to our failures.

God loves us in spite of our mistakes. If we can do the same, we shall have attained genuine self-love. Self-condemnation, on the other hand, portrays us as worthless, second rate, because of our failures. We actually hate ourselves because we are not perfect, and such self-condemnation is debilitating and destructive, pathological and un-Christian.

This pernicious disease is apparent in many perfectionists. They are always miserable, no matter how "successful" they may be; they always find a flaw. They fail to experience much, if any, satisfaction, because they are anxious about failing; when they do fail, they half expect it because they consider themselves failures. Their refusal to accept failure only plunges them into deeper turmoil. Thus they only perpetuate the cycle of perfectionism within themselves. They are hard on themselves and harder to live with. Above all, they are unable to taste the joy and peace of the Christian life generated by a forgiving God who asks us to forgive ourselves.

Self-criticism breathes new life and hope into our lives; self-condemnation brings only despair and death. For the Christian living in the shadow of the crucifix, self-criticism is relevant, self-condemnation ridiculous.

When Jesus rebuked the Pharisees for condemning the adulterous woman, he asked them to be critical of themselves.

When he spoke to her he asked her to sin no more. He suggested she learn from her failure, but above all he assured her that if he didn't condemn her, then neither should she condemn herself.

11

Self-Love

A CONFLICT OF INTERESTS?

The conflict between self-love and selfishness is so prevalent and on-going that we are not even fully aware of the tension it creates. It exists in the educated and uneducated, in the religious and the unreligious. Even clergy and religious, whom we would consider well versed in such matters, are also confused about the difference. There's much unclear thinking in this area, leading to great anxiety and to problems in people's lives and relationships.

When psychologists and Jesus tell us to love ourselves, we conclude that this is of the essence of emotional and spiritual development. Rightly so, but putting it into practice is difficult. Jesus didn't give us detailed advice, and psychologists aren't always clear or in agreement on this matter. In fact, some psychological writings can leave us mistrustful; they encourage a philosophy of "me-ism": me first and everyone else second. Therefore, most of us are cautious in acting and may often query our motives for a particular deed by asking, "Is this selfish of me?" Then, to play it safe, we may do the opposite or not act at all, neither of which is necessarily correct.

A classic example is the case of the self-giving mother and

wife who is constantly answering her children's and her husband's needs, with little concern for her own. This is the way her mother and grandmother showed love. This, she concludes, must be what the role of a good mother and wife is. To take time for herself or do something for herself would be selfish and make her feel guilty. The sad result is that she is on the way to developing selfish children and a self-centered husband, while she gradually becomes a nonperson.

Another result often unnoticed is that in the effort to fulfill the self-sacrificing role model people actually become self-centered. Their need to be loved is neurotically tied in with trying to please everyone so that they will feel loved. Since they don't love themselves, they are absolutely dependent on the love of others. Their self-esteem and identity are based on what others think of them and say about them.

There's a fine line between self-love and selfishness, and here lies the possible conflict of interests. How can I possibly love myself without being selfish? Walking this fine line and keeping a balance is a life-long task. It requires honesty, self-analysis, and a questioning of our motives. We're fortunate if we have a good friend who can help us clarify our motives or confronts us about our actions. Or we may seek counselling and come to face ourselves honestly. This is part of maturing, but it is also what lays the foundation for our ability to love another person.

One common denominator that troubled married couples have is a lack of healthy self-love and self-esteem. A loving, close relationship takes effort, and there's a strain that naturally emanates from differences in the man and woman. If one person doesn't have a healthy self-love, which includes self-respect, confidence, and belief in one's self, relating intimately will result in the following: Either the couple will be at war in order to maintain their identity, because any difference or disagreement is taken as a threat or a personal affront, signaling a lack of love; or one person will lose his or her identity by holding back and giving in, being absorbed by the other. Or there can very well be a combination of them.

In the long run, growing together becomes more and more impossible for such people, and growing apart becomes a reality. In either case, there is poor self-love because of one person's need for constant approval or a need to exercise constant control over the other. No wonder so many marriages end in divorce. Many divorced people eventually find out what true self-love is by working through the pain of a divorce. It is quite a price to pay, but it was only through the death of a marriage that they were reborn whole, recognized the gift of self, and experienced a healthy self-love.

Marriage is not so much the experience of being loved as it is the experience of loving. To be able to love means that I love myself and can handle the differences, disagreements, discord, and difficulties that any relationship involves. I shudder to hear someone say, "I feel like somebody because she loves me." In other words, "I am worthless without her love."

A healthy self-love can sustain the pain and hurts inevitable in any relationship. I may be hurt, but I'm not destroyed! Jesus said something like this: "If someone strikes you on one cheek, turn the other." If you love yourself, you can handle hurt. Many people interpret the statement of Jesus to mean that we should allow others to walk over us. You may suffer a hurt, tolerate an inconvenience, or put up with a person's quirks, but you don't allow people to abuse or destroy you. Self-love demands self-preservation!

I have often asked women, "Why did you allow the emotional (or physical) abuse you suffered from your husband?" The response was often, "Maybe he would change." But he only got worse, because she "fed" and reinforced the problem. But the other dynamic underlying this is that she didn't have the self-love, the self-respect, to stand up for herself and nip her husband's sick behavior in the bud. Sometimes a woman may even feel she deserves such treatment. That's why, when a marriage fails, two people fail.

Very simply, I need to love myself before I can love another. Our primary relationship is with ourselves and, if that's not healthy, we won't make it with another.

The central Christian theme is succinctly indicated by "Love God and your neighbor as yourself." What a splendid psychologist Jesus was! The three loves are tied together. There can't be one without the other—or the love is suspect. Sometimes we hear people talking about how much they love God, but their behavior is contradictory: they don't take care of themselves physically or emotionally.

People are always seeking criteria by which they can distinguish true love from selfish love and deal with this conflict of interests. The criteria can be difficult to describe. Here are general characteristics to help us distinguish them.

First of all, genuine self-love does what is the best for one's welfare. The best doesn't necessarily mean the easiest: what makes me feel good, or is fun, or what everyone else is doing; it often means doing what is difficult, and demanding of time, energy, or money. "The man who loses his life will find it." This often requires self-discipline and sacrifice, the ability to endure frustration now for a gain later. It frequently means facing disruption and suffering to gain greater self-recognition, not from others but from ourselves. Self-love is not just turning inward on ourselves and remaining there. That's self-centered. It means going back out, reaching out and touching others. But I must give to myself before I can give to others. I must be able to recognize my own needs before I can successfully recognize the needs of others. Genuine self-love provides us with the strength and courage to reach out to others. Jesus said, "Unless the seed falls to the ground and dies, it cannot bear fruit." The seed has to germinate and be transformed before the sprout or the fruit appears.

The Sea of Galilee receives the fresh waters of the river Jordan, and thus is a vibrant lake where fish and vegetation thrive. Then the Sea of Galilee spills from its southern outlet into the river Jordan, which flows again with fresh water and eventually flows into the Dead Sea. The Sea of Galilee is full of life because it not only receives (turns inward), but pours out and gives of itself to the river Jordan again, which flows into the Dead Sea. The Dead Sea only collects the water from the

Jordan. It gives nothing. It has no life, no vegetation. It takes, but doesn't give. This seems to me to be the key to understanding the difference between healthy self-love and selfishness. Self-love turns inward, only to turn outward to others. Selfishness turns inward and remains there—and dies. There is no outward-looking vision, only inner blindness.

So it is with ourselves. If we love ourselves we will take care and develop ourselves so we can reach out to others. Jesus fled to the mountains alone, the Scriptures state. He knew when he needed a rest, a change of pace. He was listening to his body. He knew he needed to get away, to be with himself and within himself, so he could go back out to others.

People working in the helping professions sometimes suffer "burn-out." They give to others but give nothing to themselves; they run dry. Knowing one's limitations and respecting them is good mental health. Taking a rest—a good sleep, a good meal, time out, time away—is a sign that I love myself and will be able to give to others again when I am refreshed and regenerated.

"Keep holy the sabbath day" is a way of saying, "Take a rest. Be good to yourself so you can continue to live, give, and work." Workaholics are like other addicts bent on a self-destructive course who do not take care of themselves. When parents take time for themselves and do things for themselves, they teach their children how to live and love. Good self-love provides a space to look at oneself, to reflect on one's life, behavior, and motives, to develop insights and self-understanding. This is how the working of the Holy Spirit takes place, whether through prayer or dialogue with another. This is how we get to know and appreciate the gift of self and develop that gift further. This understanding of self leads to humility; to know one's gifts means also to know one's limitations. Once we know ourselves and our limitations we can better look out at the world around us and perceive and deal with the realities of life. This self-knowledge helps us to be vibrant and productive for others.

This introspection is not to be confused with a kind of introversion, a turning in on oneself, a self-centeredness that looks only inward. This introversion lacks vision and, like the Dead Sea, it is going nowhere and giving nothing. It is narcissistic—self-centered, not other centered. It is characterized not by peace but by anxiety and fretfulness. "Why are you worried?" Jesus asks. "Look at the birds of the air. Look at the lilies of the field. They neither spin nor toil, nor do they gather into their barns, yet their heavenly Father takes care of them." Anxious people are constantly in turmoil and can't seem to break out of their own world of worries. A healthy self-love, on the other hand, practices introspection and can look out at others. It has vision, while introversion is self-serving and involves navel-gazing.

Another characteristic of sound self-love is that it is reasonable. It does not operate on feelings, impulse, or compulsion, all of which have no mind of their own. Genuine self-love bases its actions on sound reasoning. A person who loves herself is a very feeling person, sensitive, and in touch with the inner world, but not ruled by that world. In being reasonable, self-love is not controlled by a distorting guilt, or by dishonest rationalization or excuses. A person with genuine self-love utilizes his intelligence and searches for the best information or knowledge that will benefit his decisions and life.

Another lasting characteristic of genuine self-love is that it induces a sense of deep peace and satisfaction. The person with genuine self-love acts in the knowledge that he has taken all the steps and measures to do what is right, has made the best decision even in a bad situation, and is ready to stand alone in the face of peer pressure. He deals with criticism and acts out of conviction with self-confidence and a belief in himself.

This is also a description of a moral person, one who lives and acts with a sense of a deep peace and satisfaction. Thus, the characteristics of a person with true self-love coincide with the characteristics of a moral person. The less moral a person is, the less genuine self-love there is. The less moral a person is, the lower the degree of self-respect, the more self-destructive the behavior.

Peace and self-satisfaction reflect a person's values and

priorities. The worth of an individual lies within. If I love myself, my worth is in me, not in something or someone outside of me. My successes and my beautiful possessions may enhance the good feeling I have for myself and reassure me, but my basic worth depends on my loving myself. Indeed, the supreme act of faith is to believe that God loves me unconditionally as I am and that I too can love myself unconditionally as I am.

It would take a much longer essay to attempt to scratch the surface of the issue of self-love. But my purpose is to sharpen our awareness of what problems may arise when we confuse self-love with selfishness. Developing a healthy balance between them is a life-long task. Sometimes we'll succeed, sometimes fail, but to remove the conflict between self-love and selfishness is to our benefit. We love ourselves in order to love others and God. Healthy self-love is wholesome and right and has nothing to do with selfishness or self-centeredness. If we distinguish the two, we remove the uncertainty that can at times disturb us, and we can truly love God, ourselves, and our neighbor.

12

Giving

Or Giving In?

Giving is woven into daily living, an important part of relating to others. If it is to be a practical art, then we need to define what we mean by it and be more aware of it.

We may give someone a book, a ride, a pleasant glance, a dollar, a meal, or a helping hand. Or on the emotional level, we may give ourselves to others. Such giving expresses who we are, what we think, how we feel, etc. However, in our closer relationships, emotional giving becomes a much more sensitive, intense, and intricate part of relating to others. It involves not only a deeper level of sharing through communication, but also a deeper level of commitment. It is within this area that I shall reflect on three types of giving.

The act of self-giving is an act of love; it is primarily an act of the will, a decision, a choice. There can be an abundance of warm, tender feelings involved in self-giving or there can be no feelings at all or even negative feelings. But in the last analysis, with or without feelings, it is still a valid and good act.

Sometimes we naively think that when we give of ourselves it is genuine only when we have positive feelings, only when

73

we give with gracious willingness. This type of thinking leads us into trouble. Warm feelings certainly facilitate the act of giving and make it more emotionally satisfying, but when it is devoid of such feelings, or even accompanied by negative feelings, it is a much more genuine act. Giving without any warm feelings has to be based on a deep, sincere conviction; in other words, it is a deeper act of love. If we give only when we are moved by "good" feelings, our giving would be quite erratic and inconsistent, our behavior, based on feelings, would be immature and childish.

A gospel story illustrates this point. A father asks one son to go out into the vineyard to work and the son says without hesitation that he will. Then the father asks the other son to do the same thing and he, also without hesitation, indicates that he will not go. In the long run, the second son went unwillingly, grumbling, but the first son never showed up in the vineyard. Jesus asks, "Which one did the will of the father?" The answer is obvious.

If a wife asks her husband to go shopping with her and he manifests some unwillingness but then says, "For you, I'll do it," she may become irritated with him and say, "Since that's the way you feel, don't bother." In other words, if he doesn't have the accompanying positive feelings, his gesture of good will is tossed aside. It doesn't make sense, does it? The fact that he is complying without positive feelings should be even more reassuring for the wife. This is a common man/woman game. Thus, we continue to promote the erroneous thinking that self-giving is invalid or somehow counts for less unless accompanied by cheerful, positive feelings and attitudes.

In any basic commitment, we look for conviction, dedication, consistency, and loyalty. None of these characteristics require positive, warm feelings to put the commitment into effect. It is vital to understand this in any commitment, and especially in the earlier years of marriage, when romantic love, which is always accompanied by intense feelings, begins to lessen. Love is just as strong, and even stronger, when we give ourselves to another without accompanying good feelings as it is when we give with warm enthusiasm.

Because our feelings are inconsistent and not under our control, we can't allow them to govern our self-giving. If we did, commitments subject to feelings would not last because the feelings would not last. However, if I consistently lack warm feelings toward another, I would do well to closely examine my relationship; there may be unresolved negative feelings in me that need to be looked at.

In Jesus we have the illustrious example of how we might live. Jesus returns time after time to the theme that he has come to do the Father's will. His ultimate giving was his suffering and death. In his willingness to give of himself, he also experienced hesitation and fear: "Father, if it is possible, let this cup pass me by. Yet not my will, but yours be done." Here is the ultimate act of giving—without positive feelings! His self-giving came from a deep sense of commitment, conviction, and dedication.

One of the characteristics of a genuine self-giving, as difficult as it may be at times, is a subsequent deep sense of satisfaction and peace. This far surpasses the pleasing feelings that may or may not be present in the doing of the deed. Even though there may be an inner reluctance or hesitation in our giving, we are acting freely, genuinely, and lovingly as long as there is an absence of resentment, bitterness, or a feeling that we are being pressured. From our external demeanor, no one would deduce the inner struggle we may be experiencing. That is maturity! That is love!

We need to remove unrealistic and idealistic notions about "giving," or we shortchange ourselves and create unnecessary problems. However, when we speak of "giving in," that has an entirely different meaning. Giving in is a negative act. It connotes resentment, hostile resistance, being forced to do something we are unwilling to do. Such pressure can come from another person or from within ourselves. We may be acting out of fear of unpleasant consequences that may occur if we don't give in. Giving in has a flavor totally different from the willingness and conviction of giving. It is important to recognize the difference and not confuse the two so we can keep the nature of our close relationships clear in our minds.

Often, others can't recognize how we really think and feel. Sometimes, a willingness to give, with a certain grumbling, might be interpreted as implying negative resistance or resentment in the giver, while a smiling "yes" might mask underlying hostility and resentment. This latter is likely to occur when marital or family communication is not open and honest. Then people are not comfortable with each other; they are not really aware of what's happening in the other. This leads not only to disturbed individuals but to troubled relationships.

Such experiences are commonplace in families where giving in and suppressing the resulting resentment is done so well that no one realizes its presence. This may explain why, long after the childhood years, an adult harbors deep resentment toward a parent, who is either unaware of it or, if aware, is baffled by it. This may explain why a spouse just walks out of a seemingly "good marriage." Piled-up resentment has come to the surface, much of it the result of the departing spouse having "given in" for years. Giving in sabotages intimacy and leads to a false, superficial closeness: "Aren't they a loving couple? "They get along so well and never disagree or argue." Often though, this "ideal" couple has a relationship that is not genuine and is in serious trouble. Such spouses never indicated how they felt nor were they able to convert giving "in" into "giving!"

We all know the example of the little boy who never gave his parents any trouble and later even grew into a smiling, conforming teenager. Then, as a young adult, he explodes and engages in rebellious behavior. Parents are delighted to have a docile child, but very often that child is not a normal and secure child but one who hides behind a deep need for acceptance at the price of conforming and pleasing at any cost. Indeed, living with a "mouthy" teen may be a hardship but at least the parents know what this obnoxious person is thinking or feeling! His "distorted," immature behavior announces it! Giving in so as to be accepted may be a temporary solution to a problem but, in the long run such peace and conformity at any price is not only dishonest but creates emotional conflicts within the individual and eventually sabotages relationships.

Somewhere in life we all have to come to grips with the matter of giving in. In the Genesis story, Eve gave in to the serpent and Adam gave in to Eve, with disastrous results. Somehow each of us has to be able to recognize the difference between giving in and giving.

If resentment is not recognized, a great danger to good relationships occurs. Layers of resentment accumulate as a result of one party's giving in, and can be so masked that they are recognized only after unhappy consequences. Since the pattern of giving in can be as natural as breathing, it requires a conscious effort on our part to know what is going on within at all times. Total consciousness of this is not possible, but we must be in touch with our inner world as much as possible.

To solve the problem, we have to transform giving in into giving. Sometimes we shall have to express our resentment at having to give in so that the other person can read us correctly, so that we can both go on living, being tolerant with each other, compromising, or disagreeing. At least the problem has surfaced. We are no longer playing games with each other.

Such a transformation involves the individual's ability, through motivation or maturity, to change attitudes. For example, the husband who grumbles about going shopping with his wife but says, "But for you, dear, I'll do it," has transformed giving in to giving. Teens have to learn how to do this as they grow up, or they will remain immature adults. Think too of the teen who resists going to church on Sunday. Parents have to help the teen change a sense of obligation, leading to giving in, to a sense of personal responsibility, so that the teen will say, "I'm going to Mass not because I feel like it or because you, my parents, are forcing me, but because it is my personal conviction I should go. I feel a sense of religious responsibility." That's an important step toward maturity.

Dealing with our obvious or hidden mechanisms of giving in is part of emotional and spiritual growth. It means being better able to live with realistic expectations, more capable of controlling and forming our own destiny.

The ability to distinguish between giving in and giving can make a significant difference in the type of person we become in the type of relationships we form. In the end, that is basically the distinction each one of us has to make.

A great danger to good relationships occurs if resentment is not recognized, so that layers of resentment accumulate as a result of one party's giving in. These layers of resentment can be so masked they are recognized only after unhappy consequences have occurred. Since the pattern of giving in can be as natural as breathing, it requires a conscious effort on our part to know what is going on within us. *Total* consciousness of this is not possible, but we should work at being as much as possible in touch with ourselves and our inner world.

13

Compassion

HOW MUCH DOES IT MATTER?

Compassion is a theme that continually and beautifully weaves its way through the scriptures. God is portrayed as constantly compassionate, a feeling God who feels for his people, a sensitive God always in touch with them. The prophet sums up this theme: "God will again have compassion upon us (Micah 7, 19). God is not isolated or withdrawn from us, not indifferent to or uncaring about us. "God is love," St. John says, and love is caring. If we do experience isolation from God, it is usually due to the distance we feel we are from ourselves or from one another. These feelings we are likely to project onto God. In doing this, we do God less than justice, and we create unnecessary turmoil and confusion in our relationship with God. It is in such times that faith can grow, because, no matter how terrible we may feel, our awareness of God's presence is supportive and comforting.

Compassion means, among other things to reveal my feelings for what I perceive others are feeling. To show compassion is to show the apex and essence of our humanness. To be compassionate is also to be like God. Created in the image

79

and likeness of God, we are truly God's daughters and sons
when we reflect the compassion of God.

We may perceive God's grace as a powerful magnet drawing out the compassion and humanity in us. Basically we are
good, but we often fail to bring forth that goodness, to develop
that compassion for one another, which we often leave buried,
as did the servant who buried his talent and with whom Christ
was displeased.

A compassionate person is sensitive to the feelings of others,
to others' pain, joy, disappointment, fear. The compassionate
person can sense what people are feeling and express and reflect
these feelings back to them. The other person must feel and
experience or how else does she or he know of its presence?
To say "People understand how I feel for them," or, "They know
how I feel for them," without our showing what we feel doesn't
make sense. To say as an excuse for not showing how we feel,
"That's the way I am," or, "That's the way I was brought up,"
is to show a certain resistance to change, and a certain indif-
ference to others. These and other rationalizations are so many
subterfuges that let us avoid meaningful human encounters with
others, encounters that are deeply related to being Christian.

The great sin of today's world among peoples, nations, races,
indeed in all areas of human relationships, especially in our marriages and families, is insensitivity, the refusal to show feelings
and compassion to another. It is being indifferent, uncaring, and
unresponsive to the human condition of people around us. Insensitivity is at the root of the most heinous sins of our times,
for it undermines and destroys the way people should live
together, especially in families. Insensitivity to others' feelings
is more devastating than even physical abuse and is more common. Indeed, I wonder if the seeming willingness to abuse
another is not a sick substitute at times for desire to be noticed.

We often abhor the fact that there are so many people starv-
ing in today's world, even in America. Far greater, though, are
the numbers of people, in families especially, who are hurting
desperately and are emotionally starved because of the absence

of expressed compassion. This causes malnutrition of the human spirit, which is lethal to family living and loving.

Many, many people regret the absence of demonstrated affection in their backgrounds, and because of such an absence have made all sorts of negative interpretations about themselves, injuring their self-esteem and, probably mistakenly, doubting their parents' love for them. I am convinced that the perpetrators of many crimes of physical, sexual, and emotional abuse are persons who were denied compassion and sensitivity as children. The daily news is full of such tragic human stories, and behind each story, if we look and listen closely, are the pining, painful cries of emotionally deprived people, such as the sexual deviate.

The fear of being a truly emotional, expressive human person sabotages our relationships and thwarts our search for intimacy. Our relationships wither for lack of proper nourishment. Christ's description of the seeds falling by the wayside or among thorns or on rocky ground reminds us of the anemic, superficial relationships that often exist in families. The popular slogan, "Hugs are better than drugs" indicates the graphic need for family expressiveness.

People acting in a destructive manner, whether it is a student failing to take school work seriously or a spouse committing adultery, are usually emotionally deprived family members crying out for emotional nourishment. Those who ignore the pleas of family members for emotional support are contributing to the cancer that can consume even the best of families.

Listen closely to the many people you hear narrating their physical or emotional woes. They are often the victims of insensitive and uncompassionate family or marital relationships. Such people dwell in emotionally barren wastelands. Some develop psychological or psychosomatic illnesses in their unconscious search for compassion. Others endure unnecessary disappointment and frustration because there is not sensitivity for them, while others initiate nagging, conflict, and unrest to provoke *some* emotional reaction. It is not uncommon for a wife to start a fight "over nothing" (says her husband) in order to find out if he is still alive and to obtain some response from him to make sure he still cares. This kind of behavior often results from the failure of some to show compassion.

Compassion, like all human traits, has to be developed; that takes effort, work, and motivation. It exists like a raw material within each individual; it has to be mined and brought to the surface. Some of us are more aware of this than others. Much of this awareness is due to the family atmosphere in which we are reared. Was ours a "feeling family"? Did the family members *express* their feelings, their compassion, or were the members of our family emotionally restrained, too lacking in emotional expression?

It is important to realize the strengths and positive aspects of our family background, but it is equally necessary and vital that we do not fear to acknowledge the emotional poverty and limits that may have existed in it. Only then can we realize the need to develop our capacity to express as well as to receive compassion. The ability to expand this human potential is within each of us. It can and should be developed. The question is, Do we want to commit ourselves to this task? Are we willing to expend the effort required? Do we want to become more human?

The home is the arena where all learning of sensitivity has its origin. For parents to be models in expressing their feelings to each other as well as to their children, while eliciting warm and tender feelings and emotional responsiveness from them, is at the heart of family living. A sad commentary on family living today is that many parents pine over the lack of sensitivity shown them by their children. But these very same parents have failed to train their children to be sensitive to them. It is absolutely necessary for parents to indicate to their children how they feel about the childrens' reprehensible behavior or disrespectful language. When a mother says, "I feel hurt," or "I feel angry about your terrible language," she is not placing guilt trips on her children, but attempting to make them sensitive. Emotional responsiveness in families is a two-way street: parents to children and children to parents. It is a responsibility for all family members, from the youngest to the oldest. Children require training in sensitivity as they do in all other aspects of life.

To be a compassionate person also means to have a sense of sin! Sin most often involves hurting another, and depriving another of the expression of our feelings can be very hurtful. We all hear painful complaints such as, "He never made any comment on how hurt I was," or, "She never showed me any support in the job I did." To be conscious of our depriving, hurtful behavior is the beginning of becoming a sensitive person. The more sensitive we are to another's pain and the more responsive we are to it by seeking forgiveness or making amends, the more we qualify as healing, sensitive persons.

Insensitive people plow under or bruise people without any realization of what they are doing. Such persons are irresponsible, uncaring, and self-centered, and live in a world all their own, isolated from the reality of others. As people lose their sense of sin and their sensitivity to others, our world becomes a more threatening, precarious, isolated, and alienating place in which to live.

Compassion and sensitivity are an integral part of all effective counselling and psychotherapy. Hurting and troubled people seek healing, which comes not from profound intellectual answers, but from another's compassionate listening, which absorbs their pain. When people heal emotionally, they usually make appropriate decisions for their own lives and solve their problems.

One of the most effective tools for getting in touch with what others are feeling is attentive and active listening. Only by compassionate listening can we enter into and touch the spirit of another, look into the heart and mind of another. Then in communicating our sense of feeling for the other we express our compassion. In our words people feel our presence, our caring touch, our warmth, our closeness.

One person from whom we particularly expect, and need to experience, compassion and sensitivity is the religious minister. We need to feel the compassion of God coming from the caring and sensitive minister. This means the minister has to be a feeling person, not just one of words and ritual. His or her feelings will convey compassion to hurting and fearful individuals. If ministers are ineffective, it is probably because they are insensitive or fail to convey their feelings to people. Their ministry, presiding at prayer services, at ritual, at sacramental celebrations, may not be invalid but their spiritual effectiveness is compromised.

Frequently clergy (especially at services and liturgies) fail to have a "sense of people," which may be attributed basically to insensitivity. Effective ritual and preaching take place when ministers realize where their people are, what they need, what they are feeling. Otherwise, people go to the well and come away thirsty, not to mention bored and angry.

Rabbi Kushner's book, *When Bad Things Happen to Good People,* is successful and pertinent because the author reflects his sensitivity and compassion for suffering people. Whatever Jesus did, he did in an atmosphere of compassion. When we are compassionate and have a sense of feeling for others, we truly are Christian, ministers of God's compassion. Humanness and Christianity meet at the crossroads of compassion and sensitivity. People don't find God in the abstract but in the warmth of human encounters.

All the deliberations and reflections on compassion and sensitivity will never amount to much if we lack a sense of self. We must first be in touch with our own inner world—our pain, anxieties, anger, hurt, conflict, confusion, doubts, fears, all of them. Until we can experience and savor these feelings in ourselves, sensitivity and compassion toward others will never be attained. We have to be able to laugh at and enjoy ourselves, to be able to cry and be angry with ourselves, to be able to feel our own insecurity, weaknesses, and shame. One reason why Rabbi Kushner's book is so successful in touching people is that he was in touch with the intense pain and emotions he felt over the loss of his own son. Because he was in touch with himself, he could touch others.

Most people lacking compassion and sensitivity are usually not in touch with their own feelings; when they are, they are usually uncomfortable with them. What a pity that they are not able to experience the richness and depth of their own humanity. When I am compassionate and sensitive to myself, I truly experience God within me; in this experience I come to know more intimately St. John's statement that "God is love." Probably one of the most intimate ways we experience this love is when we turn to ourselves in the light of our sins, failures, and disappointments with ourselves and forgive ourselves because God loves us.

A compassionate person also must have so much feeling for others that he or she is willing to confront them. Confrontation is an aspect of compassion insofar as the compassionate person perceives that the other's behavior is hurting or destroying that person. So there is a confrontation because the compassionate person cares. The child who is letting school work go, the husband who is working excessive hours, the mother who is neglecting her health, all those not concerned about their physical and emotional well being—these and other self-destructive people need someone who senses their plight and lovingly confronts them. This may take the form of anger, discipline, challenge, pleading, or even screaming—any way we can reach them, whom we say we love. It is interesting to recognize that people in states of anxiety and depression need sensitivity and compassion, but very frequently direct confrontation is equally as necessary to dislodge or shock them out of their condition. In working with people there have been occasions when my direct confrontation, usually in the form of anger, has helped others break out of damaging habits or states of anxiety and depression. At times it was risky, but it worked.

Jesus was very compassionate, but in his compassion he felt so deeply for others that he also often confronted them: the rich young man, the woman at the well who had been "married" five times, the uneasy Peter attempting to reassure the Lord that he would not have to suffer. Moses showed his people much compassion by pleading their case before God, but that same

Moses, with that same compassion, confronted his wayward people. The prophets, with all their compassion for a suffering people, did not hesitate to confront and challenge the same people when they rebelled against God.

Compassion and sensitivity are the threads woven through the gospels and the whole of the Bible. They are the same threads we need to weave into our own lives if we are to be truly alive and human, that is, genuinely Christian.

14

Change

WHAT CAN WE CHANGE?

"God grant me the serenity to accept the things I cannot change, courage to change the things I can change, and the wisdom to know the difference." What can we really change?

This prayer is profound in its articulation of a way of life that offers hope in coping with difficult circumstances. People often feel trapped by difficult situations and they seek help from others, who may be professional counsellors or not. The key to resolving their problems is not primarily the assistance they get, but what they do with it.

People are really helping themselves when they seek help from another. People often say, "It's taken me months, years to call you for an appointment." The courage to change what can be changed starts when we realize we need help to help ourselves. Although people don't realize it at the time, it's only afterwards when they begin to understand that they were helping themselves when they reached out to an other for help. They realized they were getting back the self-confidence to tap the resources within to solve their own problems. That is what is so enabling about helping others: you don't act for them, don't make their decisions for them, don't solve their problems; you help them reach inside themselves to get in touch with their untapped and unrecognized potential.

The only thing we can change is ourselves, and that is difficult enough, but when we set out to change another, we are heading for trouble and untold frustration; people will resist if they sense we are trying to change them.

We waste so much energy trying to change others. When people squabble, especially in a marital or family situation, the complaints and accusations usually flow from the attempts of one person to change another either by threats, or laying blame, or by forcing another into submission. In these situations, the underlying message we often give is, "If you don't change, if you don't do what I want, then I won't love you for what you are because you are not what I want you to be." Here we run into the issue of acceptance, of unconditional love, that is, loving others for who they are in spite of what we don't like about them. Here we also run into the problem of the person with low self-esteem who insincerely will conform and change for another in order to find acceptance. Neurotic!

We can wait for someone to conform or adapt externally to what we want, but only individuals can change themselves internally. It will be their attitudes, values, and beliefs that will eventually affect their behavior. For example, parents have to control their children to get them to conform, but eventually and ultimately only the children's mature convictions will bring about internal change.

In an initial counselling session with a couple struggling with a marital problem, I see them locked into a bind. Neither trusts the other. They are defensive. They blame each other. They are afraid. Neither is willing to change what he or she can change. Their unhappy relationship pattern will usually begin to change when one of the spouses has the courage to do so. Always very mysterious and marvelous to see, the relationship changes when one person changes.

The one who changes influences the other in one of two

ways: by breaking up the unhealthy pattern of behavior between the two, because one refuses to take part in the games being played, ceases the power struggle, and therefore finds a new way of relating; or one person is moved to change because of the change in the other. Mutual trust is restored; the uncaring spouse becomes sincere and caring. When we change what we can in ourselves, we tend to influence others positively in one way or another. The healing power that one person possesses to change for the better in a relationship is often beyond our comprehension.

When parents are having problems with their children, I think, "Give me the parents, and they will change the children." By improving their approach to handling the children, parents influence them to act differently. It's a simple formula; it takes a good deal of effort, but it is effective. Change what we can change, ourselves, and then perhaps we can influence others to change.

Do we believe we can change? Many people have a very pessimistic view of this. They very often cover up their own refusal to change because of their inadequacy or fear of change. The critical issue always is this: "Do we *want* to change? Do we truly believe in ourselves?" This is a matter of will, of a free choice that many refuse to make.

As much as people talk about change, they sometimes fear it. We are comfortable with what we have and what we are and what our "life situation" is. It may even be a miserable situation, but in a certain sense we are secure in our misery. If we change we're not so sure what the future will bring or what we will be like. We become anxious about the situation we will be living in and so we return to what we were before or remain what we are. There is, ironically, a certain sense of security in the miserable situation, as painful as it may be.

That's why people often stay in unhealthy relationships, including marriage, because of anxiety about the future and because of their lack of self-confidence in dealing with it. In a divorce situation, the anxiety of both spouses is very high, because even though they are splitting up, the anxiety about the future can sometimes be overwhelming. It's no wonder that some people make a hasty and imprudent reconciliation to maintain a relationship that doesn't work.

People in psychological pain and turmoil scream that they don't want to live "like this" anymore, but there's always that resistance to change. It is a natural resistance, but very beneficial if we can recognize it and admit it. Then we have the possibility of being able to deal with it, understand it, and dissolve it.

Many people enter psychotherapy but when they begin to change they suddenly stop seeking help. Spouses and families plead for help, trying in some way to get relief from the agony they are in, only to back off from a new and better way of living because of the anxiety that the possibility of change produces. After their situation improves a little, they return to the "comfort" of the former misery.

Jesus once told this story: "When an unclean spirit has gone out of a man it wanders through arid wastes searching for a resting place. Failing to find one, it says, 'I will go back to the place from where I came.' It then returns to find the house swept and tidy. Next it goes out and returns with seven other spirits far worse than itself to enter in and dwell there. The result is that the last state of the man is worse than the first." I think Jesus was talking about the point that I am trying to make here.

This whole issue of change fascinates me. As I have worked with people who have changed, they have taught me much about change and growth, profoundly influencing my own way of life. I have learned that the deepest dynamic in bringing about change in our own lives is not how we change others (which we really can't do), especially those who affect us adversely, but basically how we deal with them.

I am in no way indicating that evil and injustice should be allowed to continue to exist, that we become fatalistic or passive in the face of evil and injustice, nor that we deny the obvious human tragedies that need to be eliminated from the world. But I am attempting to assert that the only power that no one can take away from us, unless we allow it, is our freedom to choose how we intend to handle our troubling life situations. In other words, we can choose to change our attitude, how we act, how we speak, how we deal with situations. We always have alternatives. As long as people or situations are overwhelming us, causing us to overreact, tearing us apart, causing unhappiness and unreasonable guilt, we are not in control of ourselves. We are being controlled by those factors; they are pulling us down. We must always come back to this awareness: "We are allowing this to happen to us. We are not dealing with the situation; it is controlling us."

Fundamental to any type of therapy with any individual, and basic to all healthy living and good mental health is the ability to ask: "How am I going to change myself in the face of this situation?" or "How will I deal with this person?" In other words, how am I going to transcend this particular problem through more mature behavior, a higher mode of action. Difficult situations can force us to grow!

Some people want to change the situation or the other person first, when in reality the only change possible is how they approach the situation or person. Perhaps then, and only then, will the situation be changed or the other person touched in some way. I have witnessed countless examples of people changing. Even though a stressful situation persists, people have been able to find peace, because in some way they were dealing with it in the best way possible at that time. Socrates said, "Know yourself!" Freud said, "Be yourself!" Christ said, "Love yourself!" Changing ourselves means that we love ourselves.

If we analyze Jesus' teaching, and look closely at his life, we see he always comes back to this fundamental issue of change: "Unless the seed falls to the ground and dies (changes), it remains just a grain of wheat; but if it dies it will bring forth much fruit." The kind of person I become is determined by how I choose to handle or not handle life's situations. We are always at a crossroads in our daily living, that is, we are constantly called upon to make choices, which determine whether we become better people or bitter people. Jesus said, "By their fruits you shall know them."

In any situation we must first look at ourselves, and then outwardly to know how we'll deal with a person or situation. This is how we maintain sanity in an "insane" world, which is always trying to control us in one form or another. This is exemplified in the experience of adolescence: being controlled by peer pressure, not being always in control of self, not thinking through, not thinking for oneself. All thinking is based on the expectations of others. Somewhere along the line we must move from adolescence into adulthood. As adults we begin to take responsibility for our lives, making choices on how we will deal with life. We may fail, but failing is also part of living. We need the courage to learn from our failures and to keep moving on, taking responsibility for our choices. Adolescence sometimes persists into adulthood because people don't want to make choices and change, taking responsibility for their own lives. They would rather sit back and moan and complain and blame. When I hear people complain about their problems, I ask, "Why don't you go and get some help?" They stop talking to me at that point: they don't want help; they don't really want to escape their situation!

Often the problems, tragedies, and unfairness of life force us to change and to grow. Part of our belief is that out of evil God can bring good, if we are willing to cooperate, doing our part in changing what we can change, ourselves. Indeed, Jesus challenges us to change ourselves: "Deny yourself; pick up your cross and follow me." He indicated that we all have to live with evil and injustice in this world. In the parable of the weeds and the wheat the servant asks the master, "Should we pull out the weeds?" The master replied, "No, let them both grow together." Jesus shows us how we are to handle ourselves in dealing with the weeds that grow around us: "Come, follow me, the way, the truth, and the life."

Jesus summons us to a new way of dealing with life. He offers other options, different approaches, new insights, a new vision, so that we can grow beyond what we were. He encourages us to be more than we are in facing the realities that surround us: "I am the light of the world. He who follows me does not walk in darkness."

When we face up to life with all its insecurities and ambiguities, we develop insight on how to deal with them. This is a gift of the Holy Spirit, who is always working in our life situations, whether we recognize this or not. The discoveries we make as to how we may alter our life in order to better cope with all of reality, whether good or evil, fair or unfair, are the work of the Spirit. But the normal way the Spirit works is through the human events and the people we experience, if we are open to life, if we filter it through our Christian principles and values, if we are reflective and prayerful about what is happening, if we are in touch with ourselves and with surrounding events. This is the faith dimension of life that assures us that God is always present, not only strengthening us but enlightening and calling us through the human pain and turmoil to further growth. As H.W. Beecher has said, "Troubles are often the tools by which God fashions us for better things."

We are constantly discerning and reflecting on what is the better thing to do, or what is best to do in a bad situation, or even, at times, what is the lesser of two evils. Our insight into the reality of what is occurring helps us to adapt, improve, or change our attitude and behavior. Sometimes the situation may call for compromising, tolerating, or conceding to the inevitability of the reality before us. There are countless circumstances that are not to our liking or quite painful. We would rather not admit that there are so many, but we should see these as challenging, even if they are discouraging.

However overwhelming our circumstances may seem to us, it's better to be honest and find some peace by accepting that they cannot be changed, but rather be courageous enough to change the only thing I am sure of changing—myself. That's the secret power and the beauty of Alanon and other similar self-help groups. They call people to change what they can change—themselves. This doesn't mean condoning evil, but accepting a new way of living with it or confronting it. It calls for a halt to being victimized by the evil. It exorcises the controlling power the evil may have over our lives. As Jesus said, "The truth shall make you free."

The essence of any psychotherapeutic change and, for that matter, the practical integration of our Christianity into our lives is to change oneself. And the better and the sooner we recognize this the more capable we are of finding a deeper sense of peace and happiness. In the long run, the painful reality of changing oneself, and learning to cope with whatever is difficult, is the basic goal in life. The realization that there is no quick answer or miraculous cure for difficult situations is the first awareness that we must come to. The real power and the answers are found within.

The first requirement in understanding the Christian view of life is that it doesn't bring miracles, but a deeper sense of viewing life, facing life, and coming to grips with life. It raises us up to a higher level beyond mere human answers, indeed to a life of resurrection—resurrection in a very practical sense, a rising from the rut of hopelessness and helplessness. As Jesus said: "I am the resurrection and the life, he who believes in me even though he dies shall live." Indeed, so often we need to die (change) before we can rise again. "The truth will make you free." Jesus is that truth. He gives us that truth. Not allowing ourselves to be controlled, overwhelmed, dehumanized, discouraged, or fall into despair because of all that is happening and because of what people are saying or doing to us— isn't this what daily death, Christian death, and dying are all about? And isn't this what it means to rise from the dead?

It means rising above the human situation, finding alternatives, changing what we can change. It means that even when we fail, there is still hope and redemption because God forgives us and we can find the power to forgive ourselves. We rise up and move on. "Pick up your cross and follow me," says the Lord, which presupposes we're going to fall. If we stop to reflect, we find that civilization always moves forward and evolves because of crises and failures that are successfully met.

The beauty of it all is that we can discover new strengths within ourselves when we fail in any way. We always seem to be able to come up with new ways of coping. One of the marvels of the human person is the ability to adjust. The old adage, "When one door closes, God always seems to open another," helps us to reach a deeper realization of God's presence in the working out of our own lives. People frequently forget, especially when up-tight, that there are alternatives.

When we look back on our lives, we realize all that we have accomplished in spite of difficulties, hardships, and mistakes. We have let go of old ways and have moved forward. We had confidence in ourselves and didn't let fear force us to maintain the status quo or hold on to the old ways, the ways that didn't work any more or were destructive.

In this connection, prayer becomes a powerful means of helping us to face life's inevitabilities, realities, and ambiguities; in prayer and meditation God is not only present, but we acquire the strength and confidence to wrestle with our many complex problems.

We discover there are no simple solutions to our problems, only reasonable answers and choices. There are no guarantees, but opportunities. Prayer helps us to focus on ourselves, but not in a condemning way. It helps us to search, to turn inward to sort out our thoughts and feelings on how to deal with a problem. Reflective prayer slows us down to consider alternative ways of acting; it prevents us from acting impetuously. Prayer is not a time for blaming others or cursing the darkness, but for coming to grips with how we are to handle the problem before us.

Pointing one's finger at others to blame for our problems is of no avail because it still leaves three fingers pointing back to ourselves, asking what we intend to do. Jesus said, "Cast the beam out of your own eye first before you try to cast the speck out of your neighbor's."

Some people consider any attempt to change as an admission of weakness rather than as a form of honesty, strength, and maturity. These people are poor candidates for any intimate relationship, since they are closed off from others and can't share their own weaknesses with another. They can't trust someone to see and accept them as they are, but, more basically, they can't really accept themselves as they are. They are rigid people, inflexible, myopic, and, to sum it all up, very insecure.

Our first, most important relationship is with ourselves. If this relationship is not reasonably intact, we are in trouble. We have to live and accept ourselves unconditionally before we are capable of loving anyone else unconditionally.

Do we have the courage and wisdom to concentrate on what we can change in ourselves? Indeed, it is the key to life. It is the key to freedom. It is the key to hope. And certainly it is the essence of maintaining peace with ourselves.

15

Roots

Do You Know Yourself?

One area of our lives we seem to take for granted is our past, especially our family of origin. We all recall incidents connected with our family background that surface feelings of joy or sorrow. But that doesn't mean that we fully comprehend the meaning our roots have for our present life. We should aim at an understanding that assembles all the puzzle pieces of our past so that we can come to a better understanding of ourselves, of who we are, why we behave, think, and feel as we do, and where we are going. In other words, we can't possibly know ourselves as we should without a fuller understanding of our family history, our heritage, our roots.

Counselling and psychotherapy, if they are to be of any value, must deal with a client's roots. In recent years this idea has been reinforced by family counselling as a means of dealing with family problems. Understanding one's present family can be greatly enhanced by the use of techniques such as geneograms, which enlighten family members about their origins.

We can't just cut off the past or deal with it lightly as an antique piece of furniture. The tragedy is that many families repeat what has happened in previous generations, even though they are appalled by what those generations underwent. Others fail to utilize the wealth of the past. Both groups of present-day families are connected to the past. As E.M. Forster once said, "Only connect!"

One of the pieces of clinical information we have uncovered is that children who distance themselves from their families to break away from them have the greatest chance of repeating the weaknesses of their families. People need to deal with the unresolved conflicts of the past at some time or they will remain and become even worse, so much so that a family background resented and rejected can actually become part of one's lifestyle. It reminds me of an inscription over the gates of Dachau concentration camp: "Those who forget the past are doomed to repeat it."

What is your recollection of your own family of origin? How realistically do you look at it? Are you able to put it in perspective? For various reasons, a great many people have blocked out all or part of their past. Very often it is because it is too painful to recall it. Those who remember only selected experiences while repressing others do themselves a disservice. Those who have a distorted picture of their family background have not examined that background realistically.

There are countless misinterpretations of the past that have been carried from childhood and never clarified. The denials and distortions of the past are heavy weights that hold a person down; they not only prevent a realistic understanding and acceptance of the past but also prevent meaningful growth and understanding of oneself as a person.

We need to acquaint ourselves with the wholesome and unwholesome patterns and scripts of living that we have carried with us into adult life; with the balanced and unbalanced attitudes and perceptions by which we now view the world; with the needs and longings never satisfied in our family of origin, needs and longings that affect positively or negatively our search for intimacy as adults.

In his "Eight Stages of Psycho-Social Development" Erik Erikson calls the last stage "integrity," wherein a person is able to integrate the full picture of her life, "roots" included, into her present life. This means that a person can look back at her past, her parents, and see that history and those parents as they were and accept them for what they were.

God's gift of ourselves is formed out of the clay of our families of origin. How we accept who we are depends on how we accept where we came from. It is always a rewarding experience to witness a person unraveling the elements of the personal, unresolved conflicts of the present by looking at the unresolved conflicts and distorted images of the past. In fact, people who unravel a present marital problem at the same time usually resolve conflicts in their family of origin, conflicts they have neglected to deal with previously, especially one with a parent with whom they had a poor relationship.

Indeed, the roots of every marital problem are embedded in the unresolved problems that people bring along with them from their families of origin. That's why I stress so emphatically with those preparing for marriage: "What you see is what you get." In other words, how does your future spouse deal, relate, and communicate with his or her own family? Patterns that you see there are the patterns and the behavior that he or she will bring into the new relationship that will be formed in marriage. But, sorry to say, in the heat of romance, lovers look only into each other's eyes and conveniently block out the view into each other's family of origin. There's much truth in the statement "Love is blind."

Why do we block out the past? One reason is a distorted notion of loyalty: we don't criticize our past. There's an illogical guilt that translates such criticism as disloyal; genuine loyalty is based on the fact that we can be realistic about our families and still accept them for who they are. Sometime in life everyone has to take responsibility to resolve the tension between loyalty to family and being his or her own person. There's a big difference between reflecting on our family and being realistic in our criticism of it and condemning that family. Socrates's oft-quoted insight, "The unexamined life is not worth living," is still true.

Another reason people fail to examine their past is that they think they won't be able to handle the pain and anger that may be buried there. Again, if one perceives anger toward a parent as wrong, then the resulting unhealthy guilt locks a person into a dark prison cell, stunting all growth. True love and acceptance take people as they are or were, not the way we imagine they should be or have been. But if we can look calmly and critically at our family of origin and accept it as it was, this, in turn, facilitates self-acceptance, self-love, and a healthy acceptance of our family, warts and all.

It takes courage to look at our family of origin, but it also takes courage to look at the way we are. In either case, we can be prevented from doing this by fear of the painful reality. But reality brings health, albeit painfully, while fear chokes off growth and maturity. I frequently request clients to write an autobiography of themselves in order to surface buried memories and feelings of their past and family of origin.

Even though we all need to examine our family of origin, this is of even greater importance for those who have emerged from damaged families. For example, if there was an alcoholic parent in the family of origin we should no longer say merely that the parent was alcoholic, but that there existed an alcoholic family and that everyone suffered and was injured in that family. Since all have been affected, all must deal with the consequences of having been bruised in such an atmosphere, if they hope to get beyond the resulting hurt and scars. It is common to trace family disorders and problems back to two and even three generations. No one in the past faced and dealt with the issues that needed to be addressed, and no one recognized (or worse, they denied) the problems in the family of origin, and therefore the problems persisted.

Let us examine two areas of our life where our experience of our family of origin has a great impact: identity and communication. First, our identity. The unique person I am has its

roots in my family background. The basic female/male iden-
tification takes place there. The family from which we are sprung
and derive our identity provides certain common characteristics
to family members, but also shapes unique individuals. Even
though we see many similar traits in family members, we also
see differences in the family members as they develop into unique persons.

The three types of families in which we fashion our iden-
tities are the enmeshed family, the disengaged family, and the
engaged family.

The enmeshed family is rigid. It doesn't allow family
members to be different; it seeks absolute conformity and control. People are meshed or lumped together in such a way that
individual identity becomes difficult to develop; there is no
allowance for individuality. It's a controlled and controlling situation. The underlying law is "conform!" There is no space, no
tolerance for one to develop individually.

In the disengaged family, the members are distant from one
another. There is a lack of interaction and cohesiveness. The
family is fragmented, with the members going in different direc-
tions. Such families often include emotionally disturbed persons,
or persons with addictions. Enmeshed families and disengaged
families have destructive patterns of relating.

The engaged family achieves a better balance between conformity and irresponsible individuality. In this type of family there
is much interaction among family members. Even though there
are problems and destructive patterns which may emerge at
times, a healthy family will correct these. The engaged family
members have a sense of security, trust, self-worth. They do
not avoid appropriate anger and fair conflict. They know how
to love and how to forgive; they relate in a healthy manner.
Are these not the characteristics also of a Christian family? This
indeed is a family that has experienced redemption. This is a
family that reflects and has integrated into its life the
characteristics Jesus teaches: love, respect, kindness,
forgiveness, understanding.

The members of enmeshed and disengaged families are

prey to excessive anxiety, self-doubt, mistrust of self and of one another, feelings of worthlessness and low self-esteem. The enmeshed family doesn't provide the atmosphere for individuals to develop or expand their unique personalities. They therefore suffer from emotional suffocation and remain unsure of themselves and immature. The disengaged family members don't nourish one another because they are emotionally distant and alienated from one another, with no sense of being loved by the others. Such families have not experienced redemption or healing.

The basic sense of identity of each child in any family is influenced by the sense of identity that each parent reflects as a person. Does the father feel good about himself as a man, the mother as a woman? Do they feel whole, secure, and confident about themselves? How do they relate and interact with each other in their roles as husband and wife? What is the quality of their relationship with their children? Implied in all these questions is the fact that the healthy or unhealthy identity of the children as persons is formed according to the characteristics the parents manifest. These are the traits that the children carry into their own lives and live out in their own relationships. Thus, the roots of each individual's identity, whether whole or fragmented, begin to develop at an early age in the family of origin.

Another important area of family life that affects our development is the quality (not the quantity) of communication in the family. Communication is, without doubt, the key to a healthy family and personality development. Conversely, lack of communication is the basic cause of marital and family problems as well as of personality deficiencies. It's not a question of which family has problems and which doesn't, but which family can communicate about these problems and which cannot. The healthy family can discuss problems and differences and thus resolve them or learn how to live with them. If the family can communicate, it can grasp the opportunities to live, to be, to become, to relate.

We learn to communicate in the family. But the crucial questions are: How did our parents communicate with each other? Did we, in our families, speak our own thoughts and feelings freely, openly, and honestly? Did we easily express our affection for one another? Were we allowed to disagree with one another? Was fair conflict appropriately expressed? How did we communicate our anger? The way we communicated with the members of our family of origin will determine how we communicate with people outside the family, especially in close relationships.

When we consider the make-up of the human person, we realize that a person's physiological and psychological being is directed toward communicating. Physiologically we are created with a mouth, tongue, facial muscles, voice box, and ears—all part of our human communication system. We are prepared to express whatever thoughts and feelings are generated within us. Psychologically, we seek closeness to others by sharing openly and honestly the deepest levels of our emotional world.

But why is that need to communicate so often thwarted, or not developed, or held in check, with the result that a healthy family life can't be achieved? We were made for revelation; God has revealed himself to us, so we also are to reveal ourselves to one another.

It takes a lifetime to develop the art of communication. It can never be taken for granted; it needs continual practice and continually needs to be re-evaluated. It means speaking from the heart and the head, so that what a person feels about himself or herself is formulated from the earliest years in the family through the communication system. How family members speak to one another, what unpleasantness they convey to one another, and how they listen to one another rightly or wrongly determines how I feel, think, and perceive myself. My image and feeling about myself may be negative or positive, but this depends on the quality of communication in my family.

From what has been said, it is clear that we have to sharpen our awareness of the importance of our family of origin and how the behavior of our family members has affected us in both healthy and unhealthy ways. It is important to think beyond the superficial dimensions of our past family history so that, among other things, we will be able to banish the fears and the guilts that keep us from knowing ourselves more fully and appreciating our past more joyfully and realistically.

I do not mean that we should blame or condemn family members but that we be able to understand them and thus accept and love who they are all the more. My intention is that we surface and then clarify and make right the countless misinterpretations that have accumulated in all of us through the years of family living, misinterpretations that have separated us from one another and prevented us from truly knowing ourselves; then we take the responsibility for our lives and move on.

Just as the Bible constantly respects people's backgrounds (notice how frequently the Scriptures describe the genealogies of individuals), we too must respect and appreciate our own family heritage, which is a gift from God. Our heritage, although ravaged by sin and failure, is also full of goodness, talent, and human potential, which is still untapped because people have failed to recognize it and so have not grown beyond themselves for generation after generation.

After reading these few thoughts, some may become pessimistic or fatalistic and conclude, "What's the use? We're trapped and determined by our past." No, we are not. The challenge we face is to grow beyond our background by understanding and learning about our families. Indeed, we can move beyond that background. We can develop its untapped riches and resources. It is a matter of motivation. This is what the Bible and Jesus call us to do: grow beyond ourselves. To the person of faith, it is possible. We hold in earthen vessels treasures far beyond our comprehension. This is what it means to be a people of hope, to be willing to meet this challenge. Isn't this what the spiritual life is all about, the willingness to grow beyond ourselves? To grow into the fullness of Christ?

As Franz Werfel writes in the introduction to *The Song of*

Bernadette, "For those who believe, no explanation is necessary. For those who do not believe, no explanation is possible." As a biblical people, we are called to change and we believe we can. Then let us not hesitate to examine the successes as well as the failures of our family of origin, whose influence lingers on in the depths of our hearts and minds.

16

Affirmation

WHY DO WE NEED IT?

We say "Amen" so often and almost automatically, especially in concluding our prayers, that it has become almost meaningless. But like most common words and actions taken for granted, it does have significance. "Amen" is our response to a prayer to which we have listened intently. By it we acknowledge the prayer contents; we were saying, "So be it; that's right, I agree." We are not only aware of the prayer itself and the message, but we approve and affirm it; we are in accord with the pray-er. However, we are too often not conscious of the importance of saying "Amen." If the one praying in the name of the group doesn't hear our response, he or she may begin to feel unsure as to whether the prayer is acceptable or not. Are the others in accord with the prayer? Therefore, the need for an affirming "Amen" in response to someone's prayer is necessary if the prayer is to be effective.

This same need of affirmation is even more necessary in human lives and relationships. We tend to travel through life not fully aware, taking much for granted, especially one another. In listening to many people, I have become conscious of their

107

everlasting need for affirmation, approval, or for some gesture reassuring them that they exist and are worthwhile. Most of the time, people don't state this need in so many words, but if you listen to the story of their life the need is apparent. In fact, the need is so evident that it is frightening in the sense that if the need is not satisfied in healthy ways, it will be satisfied in unconscious, vicarious, or destructive unhealthy ways. Some people remain chronically ill because it is a means they have found of getting attention.

The need for affirmation or "stroking" is necessary if we are to remain human and emotionally sound. We must recognize that the need exists in all of us. We need to be in touch with our inner world, in which we feel that thirst for affirmation and acknowledge it. We need to be able to accept that normal, healthy human need without considering it weakness of character, without feeling guilty or weird. It is a wholesome and good quality.

Our needs don't have a mind, and therefore our intelligence has to control how, when, and why we satisfy them; otherwise they tend to dominate and control our lives. Developing the guide of sound reason through life is part of maturing; developing an inner discipline is part of being in charge of our lives, free to choose alternative ways of satisfying our needs in healthy ways.

I cringe when I hear people say they don't need approval or make disparaging remarks about it, like "That's kid's stuff." Many people have never received that so-called kid's stuff in their families. For a person to deny such a need is tantamount to denying one's humanity. It's as senseless as denying thirst or hunger. If someone denies having sexual needs, we would say he or she is either asexual or neurotic. A person who denies a need for approval is either dishonest or very cold and out of touch with self. For such a person life would be pathological.

Sometimes our backgrounds or warped religious concepts taught us to reject such a need as unworthy of a good person, or that to want affirmation is to be self-centered and proud. This is all part of that dehumanizing approach to life that many of us learned. Our Christianity, properly understood, is supposed to humanize us and help us to recognize our needs and feelings and offer us a dignified means of dealing with them.

Scripture tells us to pray and give thanks to God. God openly approves of the praise and approval that he receives from Abel, Abraham, Moses, David, John the Baptist, and ,Jesus. Jesus constantly affirms and approves of others, such as the adulteress, who needed to know they were good persons. Jesus recognizes the human need for approval and attempts to satisfy it.

Besides the person who denies or detests his and another's need for approval, there is the other extreme: the person with an excessive need for approval and praise. To them, too much is not enough. Often these pitiable people can be very exasperating and emotionally draining, because the more praise we give them, the more approval offered them, the more they need. We can't seem to reach them no matter how much we reassure them of their goodness. They are emotionally addicted to seeking approval, sometimes at any cost. Their self-esteem and self-worth are almost non-existent.

Frequently those with an excessive need for approval come from emotionally-deprived backgrounds. Emotional deprivation is another form of emotional abuse. It's passive, but just as destructive; it's like a cancer that eats away at one's self-esteem. In the family atmosphere of emotional silence, which in itself fosters self-doubt, one wonders: "What's wrong with me?" I question my value and self-worth. The silence only magnifies my failures and the sarcasm, criticism, and disapproving nods that judge them.

The icy silence and lack of responsiveness in any relationship will lead people to make wrong and negative interpretations about the relationship. Sometimes people seek approval by acting in a negative manner, and the resulting punishment and criticism only reinforces their negative self-concept. But such people are in such need of attention that even "negative affirmation" is better than nothing, however destructive it may be.

A person craving for attention and affirmation is like an addict; there is a compulsion to find approval at any cost. There is a temporary "fix," a momentary "high," but it is never enough. The devastation of not having been affirmed as a child can leave a lasting doubt, a lasting scar on one's life.

The person who denies a need for approval probably has a background similar to the people just described, but denies and scorns the need for approval as a defense against the pain and doubt that lurk below. Families without affirmation can trace its absence back for generations. We want to ask: Won't somebody change the pattern and move beyond the past? Won't somebody begin to realize the need to affirm and approve? Won't somebody begin to realize that the human family thrives on this? And dies without it? I'm not talking about "bad" families, but about "ordinary" families. The lack of affirmation is a disorder that, even if it occurred in the past, can affect us in the present.

We still don't fully acknowledge the need for affirmation. Those who come from backgrounds that included people with psychological disorders have a great need of it. So it is the past that challenges all of us, especially within the context of our significant relationships and within our families. The one cry counsellors hear constantly is that these people were not loved, appreciated, or cared for as children, and this has left a lingering doubt about their self-worth.

Normally, it isn't that these people were not loved by their parents, because they probably were, but that they didn't feel, hear, or perceive that love in some way. The love wasn't expressed by affectionate words or deeds. It's not uncommon to hear someone say, "I know my father cared about me, but he never told me he cared." Silence is a terrible atmosphere to live in. It spawns negative or distorted conclusions or misinterpretations about oneself as well as others. And a person lives by these wrong conclusions, conclusions that lead to a negative self-image.

In counteracting such negative perceptions, it is important to develop an awareness of our basic human need to be appreciated. First of all, the awareness of this need leads us to feel comfortable with it and to possess a healthy attitude toward it. This means clearing out all the distorted thoughts and feelings about having such needs, which we have probably carried for years, programmed by our backgrounds. We have to grow beyond our backgrounds. This is not to say that our family was not a good family or that we were not loved or approved, but only that the love and approval weren't expressed sufficiently, perhaps because it was feared we would become proud if we were praised.

If we realize and acknowledge our need for approval, we will be more aware of the need of others to be approved and appreciated. They may not ask for it or indicate that they need it, but the need is there; they may even deny the need, but it is there. Even if they don't handle affirmation well when, for example, they blush or seem uncomfortable, the need is there. Our responsibility as sensitive human beings is to become more sensitive to their needs by becoming sensitive to our needs.

The next step is to put this awareness into practice—and that takes effort and even planning. This may seem artificial. After all, wouldn't affirmation come naturally? This is a false notion. Any good habit, including affirmation takes discipline to develop. Someone has to break the-family-of-origin pattern of non-affirmation that has been inherited or we will pass on the pattern to the next generation. Whenever we put some practice into action, we feel uncomfortable at first, but eventually it becomes a habit, a part of us.

As we practice affirming and approving others we are warmed by their glowing and grateful response, their smiles, their feeling good about themselves. In recognizing the good that it does to others, we reinforce the need to continue it. "Thank you," "Well done," "I love you," "Congratulations," "You're a thoughtful person," "Your grades show you are really trying"—these and many other affirming expressions are so easy to say but it takes awareness, training, repetition, and continual reinforcement in ourselves to make such a statement.

Parents, spouses, even children say about one another:

"Oh, they know I care," or "They know I am grateful and appreciate them." No, they don't, not unless those feelings are expressed! "They know I care" is one of those false assumptions we make and the result is we live with one another wondering whether the other really cares or not. The need to be expressive must be based on our convictions.

There can never be enough affirmation. If there is a balanced amount of it in anyone's life, self-esteem is nourished and this person in turn can nourish others. We have to know we are loved *and love someone else.* We live in a world that is constantly casting doubt and aspersions on our goodness. We hear deprecating statements from bitter people: "No one can be trusted," "Everyone is sleeping around," and "Everyone is out to make a buck." We all encounter normal criticism daily, justified or not. Without affirmation from those important to us we can be overwhelmed by the negative and the critical, and eventually magnify them out of proportion. When there is no affirmation of us, when the critical and the negative are all we hear, we begin to wonder: "What's wrong with me?" Furthermore, when we do affirm one another, we can be more credible when the time comes to criticize or disagree. A balance of praise and healthy criticism makes for good communication, and therefore for a good relationship.

When we affirm one another we reveal in a real and relevant manner the unconditional love that we proclaim God has for all of us. To affirm another is to put the Christian message into this hurting world in a very tangible, practical, and effective manner. God's unconditional love is manifested through people, especially when they affirm one another.

There is still one more vital aspect of affirmation, though little is said about it: the need for self-affirmation. This is a critical issue tied in with the affirmation that we receive and give. By self-affirmation, I mean we have to be honest with ourselves about the good we do, our successes and accomplishments, our good qualities. This helps us to put into perspective our weaknesses, limitations, and failures. People often take us for granted; much of the good we do or our good qualities go un-noticed. We need to feel comfortable about our need to affirm ourselves; we deserve to pat ourselves on the back from time to time. We need to thank God for who we are and for what we have. There is no better way to recognize God's gifts to us than to affirm ourselves on a daily basis.

Self-affirmation can sound terribly threatening. People in-terpret it as selfishness or self-centeredness. They suggest that the self-affirmer will get a big head and become boastful and that all sorts of neurotic manifestations will appear. Isn't this a sign of our pervasive unwillingness to believe and trust in ourselves? If we don't believe in ourselves, how can we possibly believe in the God who created us? How can we possibly believe that what God created is very good? Healthy self-affirmation is derived from a realistic self-image and from honesty with our selves about who we are.

If we affirm ourselves we are better able to reach out and affirm others. Self-affirmation is linked to the central Christian imperative of loving God and our neighbor as ourselves. "When did I see you hungry, thirsty, naked. . .?" Even if our Lord is speaking about physical needs, there is also an emotional hunger and thirst that must be satisfied: for love, affection, understand-ing, and approval.

Of Related Interest...

Healing Wounded Emotions
Audiobook
The audio version perfect for personal use as well as group use. This audiobook can be played at home, in the car or in program settings.
Three 70-min. audiocassettes, $24.95

The Pummeled Heart
Finding Peace through Pain
Antoinette Bosco
Bosco believes that pain can be a wake-up call from God, serving to shake people out of spiritual complacency and egocentric lives.
ISBN: 0-89622-584-4, 140 pp, $7.95

Psalms for Times of Trouble
John Carmody
A realistic look at life's troubles, tempered by hope for the future based on knowledge of God's infinite love and goodness.
ISBN: 0-89622-614-X, 168 pp, $9.95

From Worry to Wellness
21 People Who Changed Their Lives
Ruth Morrison and Dawn Radtke
This book offers positive, practical ways to change for the better, as demonstrated by the stories of 21 people whom the authors have counseled.
ISBN: 0-89622-443-0, 192 pp, $7.95

Available at religious bookstores or from
TWENTY-THIRD PUBLICATIONS
P.O. Box 180 • Mystic, CT 06355
1-800-321-0411